For Lady Lama the grace of God is overflowing in your life

THE MYSTIQUE OF LEADERSHIP

How to Become an Exceptional Leader

ALEX IHAMA

BALBOA
PRESS

A DIVISION OF HAY HOUSE

Copyright © 2016 Alex Ihama.

All rights reserved. No part of this book may be used or reproduced by any means, graphic, electronic, or mechanical, including photocopying, recording, taping or by any information storage retrieval system without the written permission of the author except in the case of brief quotations embodied in critical articles and reviews.

Balboa Press books may be ordered through booksellers or by contacting:

Balboa Press
A Division of Hay House
1663 Liberty Drive
Bloomington, IN 47403
www.balboapress.com
1 (877) 407-4847

Because of the dynamic nature of the Internet, any web addresses or links contained in this book may have changed since publication and may no longer be valid. The views expressed in this work are solely those of the author and do not necessarily reflect the views of the publisher, and the publisher hereby disclaims any responsibility for them.

The author of this book does not dispense medical advice or prescribe the use of any technique as a form of treatment for physical, emotional, or medical problems without the advice of a physician, either directly or indirectly. The intent of the author is only to offer information of a general nature to help you in your quest for emotional and spiritual well-being. In the event you use any of the information in this book for yourself, which is your constitutional right, the author and the publisher assume no responsibility for your actions.

Any people depicted in stock imagery provided by Thinkstock are models, and such images are being used for illustrative purposes only.
Certain stock imagery © Thinkstock.

Print information available on the last page.

ISBN: 978-1-5043-4453-1 (sc)
ISBN: 978-1-5043-4455-5 (hc)
ISBN: 978-1-5043-4454-8 (e)

Library of Congress Control Number: 2015919270

Balboa Press rev. date: 1/19/2016

Dedication

This book is dedicated to everyone who is truly committed to the essence of leadership. It is a handbook to enable you to achieve nothing but exceptionalism in your pursuit of purpose and vision.

I also dedicate this book to those in positions of authority in governments, churches, corporations, businesses, communities and schools, and offer it as a guide to help them to unlearn the Misconceptions of Leadership and embrace the Original Purpose of Leadership, the Principles of Exceptional Leaders and the Process of Leading.

I also dedicate this book to the iconic leaders that left indelible marks on humanity, particularly those who we used as examples in this book to illustrate leadership wisdom, knowledge and understanding. Some of these leaders are Jesus Christ, Abraham Lincoln, Mahatma Ghandi, Martin Luther King Jr., Rosa Parks, John F. Kennedy, Mother Teresa and Nelson Mandela.

Finally, I dedicated this book to Dr. Myles Munroe of blessed memory, for his example of exceptional leadership. I remember the impact he made on the lives of millions around the world. I honour him for the way he gracefully embraced his purpose in life with contagious passion and unwavering principles and his remarkable ability to influence those in the corporate, political, religious and academic arenas. These are the same people for whom this book is written.

Truly, Dr. Myles Munroe fought a good fight of faith and finished his race strong.

Contents

Book Endorsements xiii
Preface xxi
Introduction xxvii
Tribute to Dr. Myles Munroe xxxiii

**SECTION ONE: THE PURPOSE OF
EXCEPTIONAL LEADERSHIP** 1

1. The Misconceptions of Leadership 3
   - Misconception of Position 5
   - Misconception of Popularity 8
   - Misconception of Prosperity 12
   - Misconception of Population 16
   - Misconception of Power 18

2. The Essence of Leadership 25
   - Original Purpose of Leadership 30
   - Foundation of Leadership 33
   - Leadership and Vision 35
   - Personal and Organizational Vision 38
   - Leadership and Management 40
   - The Power of Partnerships 43

**SECTION TWO: THE PRINCIPLES OF
EXCEPTIONAL LEADERS** 45

3. The Seven Organic Laws of Leadership 47
   - The Law of Spirituality 48
   - The Law of Sacrifice 51

- The Law of Strategy 54
- The Law of Service 60
- The Law of Substance 63
- The Law of Success 67
- The Law of Succession 72

4. **The Leadership Manifesto** 82
   - Purpose for Vision 84
   - Principles for Excellence 91
   - Presence for Influence 105
   - Persistence for Progress 107
   - Passion for Life 108
   - Protection for People 110
   - Prudence for Exceptionalism 112
   - Patience for Success 114
   - Perseverance for Breakthrough 116
   - Prayer for Fulfillment 117

5. **Transformational Leadership** 121
   - Deliberate Practice 123
   - Strategic Planning 125
   - Focused Priority 127
   - Strategic Partnership 128
   - Consistent Productivity 130

SECTION THREE: THE PROCESS OF LEADING EXCEPTIONALLY 135

6. **What Leaders Often Forget** 137
   - Personal Development 140
   - Team Development 141
   - Peer Development 143
   - Corporate Development 145
   - Community Development 146

7. **Culture of Exceptional Leadership** 149
   - Original Purpose of Culture 150
   - Impact of Organizational Culture 151
   - Five Steps to Cultivate Leadership Culture 153
   - How to Sustain Leadership Culture 158

Afterword 163
Acknowledgement 167
Special Tribute to Dr. Myles & Ruth Munroe 171
About Alex Ihama 173
About Alex Ihama International 175
About School of Greatness Worldwide 183
About Welcome to Greatness 187

"Learning is not attained by chance;
it must be sought for with ardour and diligence."
–Abigail Adams

Book Endorsements

–What Exceptional Leaders Are Saying

"A job well done is the epitaph of mediocrity and the prologue of excellence."
–Unknown

"I like this book. I like *The Mystique of Leadership* because while flying at 35,000 feet it is on the tarmac at the same time. Alex Ihama has done a superb job of digging deep into the existential aspects of leadership while simultaneously staying pragmatic in his approach and application. Great stories. Great lessons. Great takeaways. Read—Learn—Grow."

– Dr. Sam Chand, Leadership Consultant,
Author of Leadership Pain,
Atlanta, Georgia, USA

"*The Mystique of Leadership* is an amazing gift from a passionate and earnest seeker who has traversed the globe in pursuit of excellence in leadership. Alex wears many caps as writer, coach, consultant and teacher. This book is a culmination of experience, theory and practice, coming together to yield a master key to unlock the timeless secrets of the world's greatest leaders. In his lucid, easily understood and reader-friendly style, the book is easily accessible to the professor as well as the common man. Give yourself this book as a gift, and then protect it. It contains a highly charged life-changing substance."

— **Professor Iyorwuese Hagher,**
Author of Leading Africa Out of Chaos,
Former Nigerian Ambassador to Canada and Mexico,
Executive Director, African Leadership Institute,
Dayton, Ohio, USA

"*The Mystique of Leadership* is a fresh treatment of a well-worn subject, as seen through the pragmatic and prismatic lenses of global citizen and leadership practitioner, consultant and catalyst Alex Ihama. Alex manages to do what few before him have been able to accomplish: reinvent and reinvigorate a time-tested genre and canon of study around which every industry, profession, organization, institution and academic discipline must grapple and come to terms with. The study and practice of leadership have developed their own body of knowledge, best practices, accepted norms, canon of literature, gurus, experts and disciples; yet Alex has asked and added several important new questions to the discussion and debate, and challenged other long-held assumptions of leadership. His approach is effectively a deconstruction of traditional, classic definitions and models of leadership, and offers fresh ideas, observations, insights and questions. I recommend and endorse this book."

— **Dr. Bruce Cook, Chairman and CEO,**
Kingdom Congressional International Alliance (KCIA)
Washington, DC, USA

"Not many books explain the rationale for leadership and compare the processes of leading in corporations, governments and churches. *The Mystique of Leadership* does. Not many books debunk the myths of leadership, unravel the misconceptions and offer leadership laws that are applicable across the corporate, political and religious arenas. *The Mystique of Leadership* does. Not many books take you to this depth of leadership and emphasize the importance of spirituality, especially in corporations, governments and schools. *The Mystique of Leadership* does. This book is a must–read for executives, pastors, politicians, professors and everyone who truly wishes to know what leadership is about. It is without hesitation, a must–read book!"

– **Sylvia Jordan,**
City Council President,
Southfield, Michigan, USA

"The author of this amazing book, Alex Ihama, penned his work for the generations yet to be born; creating a historical impact and preservation for the future. He has captured precious practical leadership principles that will serve as a compass for his generation and generations waiting to grace this earth. He has given us this valuable tool to propel us into the genetics, science and nucleic power of leadership. He provokes us into finding our passion and conviction through laws, principles and concepts that will make our lives easy, simple and truly exciting.

Whether we are in the world of science, business, politics, economics or any profession, we can use any of these practical principles in our daily lives for leaving a history to a changing world that needs it. *The Mystique of Leadership* is heaven's voice of legacy that has the power to create a history that resonate a sound for true preservation. Thank you, Alex Ihama, for writing this beautiful heartfelt manuscript that will fill the earth with hope and true leadership."

– **R. Pepe Ramnath, PhD**
Research Scientist/Author/President
Dove Environmental Laboratories
Miami, Florida, USA

"I admire the zeal and sagacity of Alex Ihama. He knows his onions and surely destined for greatness. This book is a road map for those who want to clearly understand the true concept of leadership. His style of narrative will help any reader who wants to become a leader. I have heard that knowledge is power; but in my thinking, I will rather say knowledge empowers the wise. Let this book empower you."

– **Amos Dada PhD; P.Eng.**
President, Canadian Institute of Leadership and Development &
Convener, International Gathering of Eagles Conferences
Toronto, Ontario, Canada

"Reading this book reminds me of the great opportunities generations in Africa have lost in the last 50 years as a result of bad and mediocre leadership on the continent. *The Mystique of Leadership* is a wakeup call for the next generation of leaders who desire to make national and global impact with their visions, ideas and gifts. Alex Ihama has taken the pain to chronicle his years of experience and critical lessons in his travels, speaking and consulting engagements as well as his associations with the people I call the 'critical few' and have made them available to us all. Great insights based on principles and rare revelations that have proven to be the most effective genre for servant leadership. *The Mystique of Leadership* is for those who seek to be leaders at home, work and in their countries."

– Emmanuel Dei-Tumi
CEO, The Future Leaders Group
Accra, Ghana

"Alex Ihama is a new generation coach, trainer, speaker, consultant and writer. My first encounter with his book and teachings revealed a thorough astute, diligent and focused leader. Alex Ihama is a go-getter with very flaring leadership qualities; you can't dream of a better mentor. To buy this book however means to receive double blessing since the book itself is dedicated to Dr. Myles Munroe, who was one of the most competent human developers of our generation. This combination of wisdom and insight from Dr. Myles Munroe and Alex Ihama will greatly enhance your leadership potential."

– Pastor Sunday Adelaja,
Senior Pastor, Embassy of God Church,
Kiev, Ukraine

"This is a classic! Simply put: the title says it, the content explains it, and the conscientious reader can now apply it! This work appeals to the construct of so many minds-that of the philosopher, the psychologist, the sociologist, the businessman, the clergy and the academician. In *The Mystique of Leadership*, Alex Ihama neatly juxtaposed the principles of theory with the evidence of praxis based on his extensive research, iconic references, keen observation, personal experience and intellectual analysis. In this masterpiece he has invested into the future, the legacy of a leadership culture which will become for me personally, a professor's dream text, a mentor's manual and a practitioner's plum line. Thanks Alex, I will treasure this".

**– Dr. CB Peter Morgan,
President, International Third World Leadership Association,
Nassau, Bahamas**

"*The Mystique of Leadership* amplifies the leadership purpose to develop others and anchors it on a simple spiritual norm of 'respect for people'. In this book, Alex Ihama inspires those in positions of authority to engage, enable and empower others to become increasingly self-reliant".

**– Carmen Puzzo,
Senior Vice President (SVP),
Canadian Imperial Bank of Commerce (CIBC),
Toronto, Canada**

"In *The Mystique of Leadership*, Alex aligns complexity with common sense. In the process, he simplifies and demystifies a myriad of myths, mysteries and misconceptions about leadership. With convincing clarity fostered by his characteristic clear constructs and coinages, Alex uses this book to delineate, define and discuss the dogmas and doctrines that are rightly or wrongly associated with leadership, while making a compelling case that the application or misapplication of these dogmas and doctrines has drawn dividends or drown dreams respectively for dozens of decades.

In *The Mystique of Leadership*, Alex is not content with mere theoretical thesis—in respect of which he draws relevant references from the rich repositories of time-tested thinkers and leaders—as he, armed with his trademark truth–be–told tenacity, delves into real life experiences and offers clarity, clear–headedness and survival strategies to anyone who is trapped in or perplexed by the polemics of the "leadership" language. Alex accomplishes this feat by situating the successes or failures of biblical figures, iconic individuals, conglomerated corporations and countries within the contexts of the strategies that he simultaneously unravels in the book. Alex thus demonstrates, in one breath, that he is an astute advocate of axioms and a professional practitioner of practicality.

One of the most gripping, instructive and impactful sections of *The Mystique of Leadership* is Alex's introductory tribute to Dr. Myles Munroe, the late iconic minister and motivator. In a telling tribute, Alex provides a historical account of how *The Mystique of Leadership* was birthed by a combination of both his inborn quest to question, debate, debunk and demystify the myths and misconceptions about leadership and a dogged determination by him to fulfill Dr. Munroe's motivational mantra for one to "die empty"! In chapter after chapter that follow the Introduction, Alex seamlessly takes the reader through both familiar and unfamiliar territories with a resultant magnetic, meaningful and constant connectivity between the reader and Alex's messages in the book. This makes *The Mystique of Leadership* an easy, breezy and refreshing read.

The Mystique of Leadership concretizes and reinforces the axiom that any man who minds and mines his mind will not fail to find that he is a rich reservoir of inexhaustible ideas. It unapologetically unleashes the truism that when a man mixes spirituality with his God–endowed intelligence, he awakens the deepest parts of his essence, he is able to imprison his imperfections and fetter his fears and he exponentially elevates every effort he makes towards confronting the constant challenges of life, thereby expanding his chance of survival and success. It draws the irrefutable inference from a thorough thought–process that nobody should aspire to–or be entrusted with–a position of leadership in any sphere of human undertaking–be it academic, political, financial, moral or religious–while devoid of spirituality.

Aside from the certain impact that *The Mystique of Leadership* will have on the group it expressly targets, namely, those who occupy leadership positions. I am convinced that this epic book offers life–altering strategies to all: from the cleaner to the cook to the chief executive officer and from the atheist to the altar boy to the priest. The book will inspire everyone to aspire to leadership or remain in leadership provided that they first "learn, unlearn or relearn" in line with the robust roadmap it offers. It simply searches for—and speaks to—your senses and your soul! It is a manifestation of why Alex Ihama is respectfully regarded as a topmost igniter of intense intelligence."

> **– Kingsley Jesuorobo, Barrister, Solicitor & Notary Public,**
> **Principal Counsel, Kingsley Jesuorobo and Associates,**
> **Co-founder and Director, FEVA TV,**
> **Toronto, Canada**

I am truly honoured to endorse this empowering book as it is yet another outstanding leadership contribution to this generation by its author Mr. Alex Ihama. Alex is a very intelligent, strategic, and wise leader that has taken the time to pen his thoughts, strategies, and personal experiences, giving this generation the opportunity to glean and apply time-tested principles he has observed, learned, and applied.

The principle I appreciate the most from this book is the principle of honour, illustrated in the tribute to my spiritual father, mentor, and significant world impactor, the late Dr. Myles Munroe. Alex has made significant effort to acknowledge the impact Dr. Munroe had in his life and has sown a seed that will reap the harvest of such a great honour. This book will equip you for your next level of success along the path of destiny. Therefore, as you prepare to consume this well-prepared leadership manual, I invite you with the greetings of the author's previous book: "Welcome to Greatness!"

> **– Dr. Stacy LeMay,**
> **Senior Pastor, Champion Kingdom Centre,**
> **Charlotte, North Carolina, U.S.A.**

A long needed and well thought-out exposé on practical leadership nuances that very few authors have attempted to address. In his book, *The Mystique of Leadership*, Alex Ihama de–mystifies, in a very detailed manner, many of the grey areas on the subject of leadership. This will help leaders from any background or industry to harness the skills needed to transform people's thinking and attitudes, starting with their own. The real-life stories in the book help to drive home the point. Ihama's book is a must read for corporate leaders, pastors, community and youth leaders, mentors, parents, and anyone seeking to improve themselves, as well as inspire others to achieve greatness! Alex's reminisce on the life and exceptional leadership of Dr. Myles Munroe is to say the least, awe-inspiring!

– Pastor Ghandi Olaoye,
Senior Pastor, RCCG Jesus House,
DC Silver Spring, Maryland, USA.

Preface

Case for Clarity

> "The illiterate of the 21st century will not be those who cannot read and write, but those who cannot learn, unlearn, and relearn."
> – Alvin Toffler

Is there really a need for another book on leadership?

I wrestled with this question for many years until I realized that the standard of leadership in many companies, governments, churches and colleges is lagging and an increasing number of people are assuming positions of authority with insufficient leadership skills. A simple Google search on leadership returns about half a billion hits in a quarter of a second. How can any person in a position of authority discern the true meaning of leadership with such results? No wonder why so many leaders do not understand the fundamentals of leadership.

The need for stronger leadership is so strongly felt today that some question if the world will ever witness again the exceptional leadership of such icons as Jesus Christ, Abraham Lincoln, Mahatma Ghandi, Martin Luther King Jr., Mother Teresa and Nelson Mandela? Could the passing of President Nelson Mandela in 2013 have really marked the end of exceptional leadership? Is there anyone among us with the same vision, wisdom and courage to inspire the level of spirituality, sacrifice and service as those notable leaders of the past?

With so much information on leadership, where do you even start? How do you even decipher what is important, accurate and applicable leadership qualities these days? What can possibly be written today about the concept of leadership that has not been written before? What was the original purpose of leadership in the first place? How and why have the fundamentals of leadership changed over time? Why is such a basic concept so misunderstood by many, including those who spent years studying it at higher levels of education?

I have been studying and speaking on leadership for almost two decades and have held different leadership roles within profit and non-profit organizations. I have coached and been consulted by corporate executives, global entrepreneurs, political appointees and religious ministers on how to become an exceptional leader.

Many of them possessed enormous influence, but were unable to inspire people to achieve their maximum productivity. They honourably aspire to advance their vision, yet were unable to empower their teams to use their skills and talents to advance a common vision. These leaders spent great effort to achieve profitable growth, but were unable to motivate their teams for personal and organizational success.

As I examined each of their challenges, the more apparent it became to me that the essence of leadership has been diluted over time, while the characteristics for which exceptional leaders are known had become too convoluted for people to understand. I also discovered that for generations the process of leading has been mostly approached from a corporate perspective, regardless the type of organization or groups of people attracted by the vision.

In short, some people were no longer aware of the original purpose of leadership and were confused by the myths and misconceptions about it. I realized that this lack of awareness indicated a dire need for leadership clarity in governments, corporations, churches and schools.

It was alarming to realize how the meaning of leadership varied depending on the vision, mission and passion of those who were in positions of authority. Amazon has nearly 30,000 direct titles and almost 100,000 indirect titles on leadership; however, many of these books only offer the same information about leadership from the same perspective. They share lots of information on the 'how', but not enough on the 'what', 'when', 'where', 'why' and 'why not'.

The Mystique of Leadership explains the rationale and original purpose of leadership. It compares the processes of leading in the corporate, political and religious worlds and debunks the myths and unravels the misconceptions about it. It offers a set of leadership laws that is applicable across corporate, political and religious sectors, while emphasizing the centrality of spirituality.

This book summarizes very important leadership concepts into easy-to-follow, step-by-step processes and frameworks. It is written as a handbook for everyone, especially those who are in, or who aspire for, positions of authority in corporations, churches, schools, community, and government.

The Mystique of Leadership is a comprehensive and succinct summary of the essential things that you must know about leadership while revealing the answers and solutions to longstanding questions about leadership. It uses real life stories and case studies to equip you with the knowledge and strategies to enable you to become an exceptional leader, while introducing you to frameworks to help you build and sustain leadership culture in your organization.

This book will challenge your mindset, compel you to action and inspire you to be and do more personally, professionally and universally. It is a framework for exceptional leadership and a roadmap for personal success.

While the book will benefit anyone seeking to learn the true meaning of leadership, I address those in positions of leadership in corporations, governments and churches and those who aspire to leadership roles. It is a personal guide to help you unleash the leadership capabilities within you.

It is a curriculum for leadership training in your corporations, colleges and churches, and a handbook to instigate paradigm shifts and cultivate a leadership culture in governments, communities and associations. This book will captivate the persistent, challenge the persuasive and compel the unrealistic.

I write this book at a time when executives desperately desire the trust of their employees and the loyalty of their customers. I write this book when citizens are praying fervently for relief from the ineffective leadership of their politicians or the outright dictatorship that has held them captive for generations. I write this book when students and congregations are looking up to their teachers and pastors expectantly for consistent information and constant inspiration.

I write this book at a time when many seek to understand the relationship between church and state, when the truth must be told in the face of political correctness and when morality must be advocated in the face of pop culture. Nothing is more exciting than to realize the enormous opportunities that still exists to equip those who are in positions of authority and empower those who long to ignite their leadership spirit.

Is there really a need for yet another book on leadership?

Absolutely! There is an urgent need for the type of clarity that this book offers.

Despite the depth of leadership knowledge that is available to us today, I was amazed by the amount of wisdom that was revealed during the process of navigating through the haze and maze of it all. While I applaud the outstanding efforts of renowned teachers such as Peter Drucker, Stephen Covey, Dr. Myles Munroe, John C. Maxwell, Ken Blanchard and Robin Sharma, *The Mystique of Leadership* addresses the essential components of leadership where clarity is required and practicality is desired.

I draw from the lives of iconic leaders to inspire the leadership spirit of our readers while confronting the myriad of myths and misconceptions that confound the essence of leadership.

Outlined in the form of a roadmap, a personal journey through the labyrinth of leadership, this book will enable you to see how the meaning of leadership, one of the most challenging concepts of our time, really can be easily understood. You will begin to clearly see the habits of leadership that you must unlearn in order to become an exceptional leader.

I have been using the knowledge and strategies in this book to ignite the spirits of leadership and entrepreneurship in many people for decades. Now I succinctly summarize my message to enable you to do the same for yourself. This book will compel you to think and look beyond what you know and see to discover the true essence of leadership.

The Mystique of Leadership contains real life stories of iconic leaders of the past and innovative leaders of today: corporate executives, community advocates, politicians, billionaire entrepreneurs, religious gurus and academics. You will learn how to leverage the principles, strategies and frameworks that made them exceptional in leadership. You will discover how to leverage our vast philosophical, physiological, spiritual and psychological research to achieve success in your personal and professional endeavours.

Whether you are in a position of authority or not, this is the handbook you have been waiting for to ignite your leadership spirit. It is a reference guide that will enable you to lead at your best, a compelling narrative to motivate and empower you to take the baton from the hands of iconic leaders.

The Mystique of Leadership is a roadmap for self–discovery, awareness and actualization. You can apply it in every aspect of your life. Read it with an open mind and a heart that is yearning for change–personal, corporate, political, academic and religious. Embrace it with the same sense of urgency in which it was written so that you may be possessed with an even fiercer urgency to inform, influence and inspire others.

If there was ever a time to go back to the basics of leadership and begin the transformation of mindsets around the world, it is now. You are the leader you have been waiting for and it is our honour to be your guide.

Welcome to Greatness!

Introduction

Summary of Framework

"The dogmas of the quiet past are inadequate to the stormy present. The occasion is piled high with difficulty, and we must rise with the occasion. As our case is new, so we must think anew and act anew."
– Abraham Lincoln

Mystique describes a framework of doctrines about a belief, person, place, idea, thing or any concept with deep meaning. It endows upon whatever is being described a profound significance, wonder and heightened value.

The Mystique of Leadership, therefore, is a framework that was delicately put together to empower you with the critical concepts and precepts required to be an exceptional leader. It reveals the qualities that make leadership exciting, the aura of mystery, awe and power that surrounds it, and the esoteric skills that are essential to be exceptional in it.

This book is a summary of many great books on personal and leadership development, and organizational success. It is a condensed version of what everyone must know about leadership, particularly those in positions of authority or aspiring to them.

Since the heightened complexities and competiveness of today has created difficult challenges that can only be curtailed by exceptional leadership, it is imperative that everyone, whether in positions of authority or not, become aware of the original purpose of leadership. It is crucial that we deepen our understanding of the natural laws that govern leadership, the prerequisites for exceptional leadership, characteristics of exceptional leaders and how to build leadership culture in our communities, homes, work, places of worship, governments and schools.

Now is the time to unravel The Mystique of Leadership.

After speaking to audiences worldwide for two decades on personal and leadership development, I realized a dire need to debunk the prevailing myths and misconceptions of leadership. I realized that the overwhelming leadership information on the internet creates an urgency to discern whether leaders are born or made. It challenges us to consider the essence of leadership, the principles of exceptional leadership and the relationships between purpose and vision, vision and leadership, and leadership and management.

It was obvious that the leadership frameworks and models of the past, however fruitful they were, are now out-dated, if not altogether detrimental to understanding leadership. I concluded that those who wish to be exceptional in leadership must begin to think and act anew.

The Mystique of Leadership is a roadmap for your journey back to the basics of leadership. In this journey, you will discover the original purpose of leadership, the roles and responsibilities of an exceptional leader, the importance of leading exceptionally and how to successfully advance a vision. You will learn about the predominant leadership challenges in corporations, governments, churches, communities and schools, what makes leadership to be ineffective and eventually dictatorial and how you can rise above these challenges to become an exceptional leader.

To make this framework easy to understand, I break it down into three main sections: The Purpose of Leadership, The Principles of Exceptional Leaders and The Process of Leading Exceptionally. Everything you need to know about leadership, whether in this book or not, falls under one of those categories.

The book begins with a special tribute to Dr. Myles Munroe, who was widely respected in the corporate, political, academic and religious sectors as an exceptional leader. Besides being inspired by him to write this book, I realized how exceptional he was in leadership as I wrote this book, and how possible it actually is for anyone to become an exceptional leader as well.

Based on his life, and the lives of iconic leaders such as Jesus Christ, Abraham Lincoln, Mahatma Ghandi, Martin Luther King Jr., Mother Teresa and Nelson Mandela, *The Mystique of Leadership* outlines the commonalities and characteristics of exceptional leaders, regardless of race, gender, socio–economic status, religious beliefs and academic background. It must be read carefully and kept handy as a reference guide forever.

It is essential you read through the Preface, Tribute, Endorsements, this Introduction and the Afterword at the end of the book in order to ensure that you have all the pieces of this leadership puzzle; parts which most of the world is still trying to figure out. Each chapter-and some sections within the chapters-begin with a quotation that best summarizes the intent and content of that passage.

Reflect and meditate carefully on them and take notes along the way, capturing every nugget of wisdom and the questions you may have. Know that what may be unclear in the beginning of the book will likely become apparent somewhere along the journey. Without a doubt, you will be transformed as you proceed prudently and patiently along the way.

Each chapter contains a wealth of information and should not be rushed through like a novel. Enjoy the opening quotations, applicable analogies, inspiring biographies of iconic leaders and the company case studies. Reflect on whatever resonates with you and meditate on those things until you realize the infinite possibilities in your own life as well. Consider this as an expedition to the core of your existence, a voyage in which you are the driver and the passenger.

While this book can be used as a curriculum to facilitate leadership training in corporations, colleges and churches, it is a personal guide to unleash the leadership capabilities in you and a handbook for cultivating a culture of leadership in homes, governments, communities and associations.

The chapters in the first section of the book—The Purpose of Exceptional Leadership,—focus on what leadership isn't as well as what it is. Instead of offering an uneven perspective of leadership, I approach each topic from what it isn't, what people think it is, why some people in positions of authority struggle with the topic and how to renew your understanding.

I use this approach to compare and contrast modern thought about leadership with its original meaning. This is another reason why I recommend that you read this book purposefully, passionately, persistently, prudently and patiently, which are five of the ten characteristics that make up The Leadership Manifesto in the second section of this book.

In addition to referencing exceptional leaders like Bill Gates, Steve Jobs, Michael Bloomberg, Aliko Dangote and Mark Zuckerberg, you will also be introduced to emerging leaders like Jan Koum, who left Yahoo to co–found WhatsApp Inc. in 2009 and later sold it for $19 billion to Facebook Inc. You will hear the story of Elizabeth Holmes, the 30-year-old woman who dropped out of her sophomore year in the prestigious Stanford University to begin a blood testing company in 2003, later rising to Forbes's list of billionaires.

You will meet Tony Elumelu, a self–made billionaire entrepreneur from Nigeria who recently pledged $100 million towards creating 10,000 entrepreneurs across Africa in the next ten years. Finally, you will read the story about Dan Price, who, with his brother, founded Gravity Payments in 2004 at the age of 19. He was honoured six years later by President Barack Obama as the National Young Entrepreneur of the Year for his success.

In this framework, I take a strategic approach of specialization in leadership development, highlighting the necessary skills for you to work on depending on your capacity of leadership. As a result, I break down leadership into spectrums, with our primary focus on Corporate Leadership, Political Leadership and Religious Leadership. While the concepts and precepts are applicable across the board, including in Academic Leadership, Community Leadership and Youth Leadership, your leadership spirit can only be sustained when you are in a field that perfectly aligns with your purpose in life.

This is why I cover the topic of purpose extensively throughout the book. Just as certain species of fish can only thrive in certain parts of the sea, so too can we only thrive as leaders in our particular calling, the work where we are excited the most. As you will learn in this book, leadership is based on purpose, and purpose determines your spectrum.

Regardless of your education and experience, you will be captivated by how ordinary people became exceptional leaders in their areas of calling. You will be challenged by how much you need to unlearn and relearn, and compelled by the encouraging fact that to become an exceptional leader is mainly based on personal decisions, regardless of your situation or position in life.

So get ready to be equipped with the wisdom, knowledge and understanding that will enable you to become the exceptional leader you desire others to be. In the words of Albert Einstein, "We cannot solve problems by using the same kind of thinking we used when we created them." *The Mystique of Leadership* is bound to empower you to correct the thinking that led you to your current situation; and when completed, completely renew your mind altogether.

I wish you nothing but the very best in this exciting journey of personal transformation, leadership development and organizational success. While I applaud your courage for allowing yourself to be challenged, for being so open to learn, I am excited for those around you who will equally benefit from your renewed mind and spirit.

Whether you are a corporate executive, entrepreneur, politician, pastor, teacher, community advocate or a professional of some sort, we are all students of life. *The Mystique of Leadership* will enable you to increase your capacity for even greater achievements in life. If there was ever a time to become an exceptional leader, it is now.

With *The Mystique of Leadership* in your hands, the world waits in eager expectation for you to be revealed.

Tribute to Dr. Myles Munroe

An Exceptional Leader

"Leaders like Myles and Ruth Munroe teach us that we are our brothers' and sisters' keepers, and challenge us to practice what we believe through deeds as well as our words."
–President Barack Obama

A few years ago, the consistency with which I advanced the vision of our School of Greatness worldwide created the urgent need for me to seek strategic advice from a few people who were further along on the path. I made a list of qualified Global Leadership and Management Consultants that I would be very honoured to associate with, people who inspired me and from whom I wanted to learn.

There were a handful of experts who were resourceful and relentless in the pursuit of their purpose, a few people who were running their race with so much focus and faith that their messages were transforming the mindsets of people all over the world. They were exceptional in leadership and enabling others to be and do more for the world. I prioritized the list and made the effort to reach out to them one by one.

At the top of my list was Dr. Myles Munroe. His crystal–clear focus on his purpose, his contagious passion and blunt refusal to negotiate his unwavering set of principles drew me. He was single-minded in his purpose and faith in God and in himself to the extent that he was no longer bothered by the fear of anyone or thing, including death. It was clear to me that Dr. Munroe had not only discovered his purpose in life, but lived it with what Martin Luther King Jr. once referred to as "the fierce urgency of now."

Without a question, Dr. Munroe achieved self-actualization and was apparently in the last leg of the race marked out for him; a race that we are all called by God to individually run with perseverance. Indeed, Dr. Munroe was living life to the fullest. He was an exemplary and exceptional leader.

I bought and read most of his 69 books, watched about a hundred of his videos on YouTube and devoured his online articles and social media postings. Everything that I studied, watched and listened to compelled me to connect with him with the hope of him becoming my mentor. I researched when he would be in his hometown of Nassau, Bahamas.

I purchased a vacation package and went off to meet one of the most travelled speakers on the planet. I was off to meet an exceptional leader, who, for almost 40 years, had been speaking directly to half a million people each year in corporations, churches, communities, colleges and governments worldwide.

I arrived in the Bahamas on a Friday, visited the city on a Saturday and was the first to arrive at his church on Sunday morning. In fact, I patiently sat inside the taxicab waiting until the doors to The Bahamas Faith Ministries International (BFMI) opened. I approached a member of the church staff, introduced myself and told him why I had travelled all the way from Canada. The gentleman was amazed when he found out that I was not just a tourist seizing the opportunity to meet Dr. Munroe. He took me to the front and offered me a chair right behind where Dr. Munroe would sit during the service.

Right after Dr. Munroe spoke that morning, I gave him a hug. I could see that he was trying to recollect from his vast memory if we had previously met. I quickly introduced myself and told him why I came to the Bahamas. That afternoon, I was at his home having lunch with his family and a group of his associates.

It was there that I learned the most powerful lesson in my life: be so secure in yourself and your purpose in life that you are open, hospitable, gentle, generous and welcoming. This lesson came alive before me in the person of Dr. Munroe. I felt it and experienced it in a way that no book could teach me.

Dr. Munroe worked on himself so hard and was so transformed that he was threatened and intimated by no one—not even by death. He said and demonstrated this all the time. His positions on social, political and religious matters were explicit, even when they were unpopular or provoked those in positions of authorities in governments around the world.

He gracefully embraced his purpose in life with a contagious passion and firm principle, and yet he possessed the rare ability to influence both the corporate, political and religious worlds. He influenced younger generations in schools, as well as elder statesmen. He was welcomed in the hearts and homes of millions of people, and was invited to speak at the prestigious Harvard University.

In his tribute at Dr. Munroe's funeral, Dr. Joel Edwards, the International Director of Micah Challenge, said, "Dr. Myles touched so many lives on so many issues across so many communities. He was comfortable with Prime Ministers as he was with the people; he walked with kings without losing the common touch. The world mourns the loss of a man who revealed the mind and heart of God."

Dr. Munroe was the country's youngest recipient of the Queen's Birthday Honours' Order of The British Empire (OBE) Award, which was bestowed upon him in 1998 by Her Majesty, Queen Elizabeth II, for his spiritual and social contributions to the national development of the Bahamas.

My speaking engagements have taken me around the world and offered me opportunities to meet people in high levels of authority, people with enormous influence. But never had I met a man like Dr. Munroe, a man so authentic and accessible to everyone at every possible opportunity.

Many tributes alluded to the personal attention that he gave to every encounter with people. People spoke of how he was able to make everyone feel important and how he consistently expressed appreciation even for the things entitled to him. Indeed, Dr. Munroe was an exceptional leader.

At his funeral, some of his business associates shared how he never refused to give an autograph or take a photograph with anyone, anywhere and anytime. So great was his dedication and attentiveness to others that there were occasions where he and his group missed international flights. He firmly believed that leaders should always make themselves available to people as much as possible, even at their own inconvenience and expense.

His habit of constantly putting people first, of consistently making extra efforts to inspire everyone along his way and to be fully present in every encounter were the things that made Dr. Munroe such an exceptional leader.

I met with him again on the next day. Surprisingly, he had reviewed a copy of my book *Welcome to Greatness* which I gave to him during dinner the previous day. He referred to parts of the book that impressed him the most, and surprisingly, offered to write a foreword for the next edition of it or any other book that I intended to write. He praised my book *Welcome to Greatness* and freely shared ideas for maximizing the wisdom in the book and to extend its impact. Just as he was deeply spiritual, so was he consistently strategic in his approach to people and events.

I was amazed to realize that one of the busiest people on the planet made the time overnight to review a book that was given to him by a total stranger. Not only that, he also took the time to provide in-depth feedback. Due to the overwhelming distraction of our days, responsiveness is a rare trait to find in leaders today.

It is a trait that makes leaders exceptional, and Dr. Munroe obviously excelled in it. Indeed, he was determined, dedicated and devoted. He was absolutely committed to the development and advancement of everyone, as any exceptional leader should.

It was during this visit with him that he challenged me to travel around the world with my inspirational messages on greatness, purpose and leadership. He encouraged me to focus on those who need to hear these messages the most, especially in developing countries. He inspired me to neither relent nor tire and to keep pressing onwards, no matter what. This man said so many things that my life changed in the few days that I spent with him.

What I learned from him heightened my aspirations and impacted the lives of my family, friends and associates forever. In only a few days, Dr. Munroe made a major difference in the lives of those he would never meet through an encounter with me.

Due to the intensity of the training, coaching and mentoring I received from him, coupled with the excitement of learning so much in so short a time, I left the Bahamas without having time to sit and sip on a cocktail by the beach. I came back to Canada with an enlarged vision, a revolutionized spirit, an unequivocal sense of urgency, and an unquenchable determination to heed the advice he gave in his autograph: "die empty."

His ability to get people in touch with themselves and ignite higher levels of passion within them was another rare quality that made him an exceptional leader. Globally renowned as a bestselling author, lecturer, teacher, life coach, leadership and government consultant, he was also a musician, trainer, entrepreneur, pastor and nationalist. And now, he was a friend and mentor to me.

On October 22, 2014, he sent me a message from Dar es Salaam, Tanzania, to say he was looking forward to seeing me at his annual Global Leadership Conference, which was scheduled to take place on November 10, 2014, in Freeport, Bahamas. I responded immediately and conveyed my regrets that I was unable to attend because of a prior commitment to be the keynote speaker for the sales convention of a major financial institution in Toronto, Canada. Besides, both of us were scheduled to speak at a major leadership conference in Port Harcourt, Nigeria, in March 2015, and I would see him then.

Unfortunately, the private aircraft that was flying him and his wife, Lady Ruth-Ann, to the conference, crashed while attempting to land at the Freeport airport on Sunday, November 9, 2014. There were no survivors. Onboard the aircraft were seven other people, including his closest friend and partner in ministry and business, Dr. Richard Pinder.

Others aboard the plane were Farkhan Cooper, Captain Stanley Thurston, Diego DeSantiago and Pastor Lavard Parks, the leader of his youth ministry. Pastor Parks' wife, Radel, and his son, Johanan, were also on the flight. This was not just a tragic loss to Dr. Munroe's family, particularly his two children, and his organization, but indeed, to the Bahamas and the world.

According to the Prime Minister of Bahamas, the Rt. Hon. Perry Christie, "It is utterly impossible to measure the magnitude of Dr. Munroe's loss to The Bahamas and to the world. He was indisputably one of the most globally recognizable religious figures our nation has ever produced. His fame as an ambassador for the Christian ministry preceded him wherever in the world he travelled, whether in the Caribbean, North America, Asia, Europe or Africa. He was a towering force who earned the respect and admiration not only of Christian adherents but of secular leaders both at home and worldwide."

The Prime Minister of Bahamas revered Dr. Munroe as "a man who never forgot his roots; a man who was passionately involved in Bahamian nation–building and who played an important part in that process over the course of more than three decades. So, let us make no mistake about it therefore, while Dr. Myles Munroe was unquestionably a globalist, an internationalist, in scope of his Christian ministry and in the reach of his teachings and travels, he was at the same time a profoundly committed nationalist; a Bain–town–bred Bahamian through and through."

Dr. Munroe's ability to make his message relevant to everyone led him before kings and presidents and paved way for him wherever he went. His life was an absolute attestation to King Solomon's proverb that a man who is skilled in his work will indeed stand before kings and not stand in front of obscure men. He dedicated the latter years of his life to coaching, consulting and mentoring heads of states all over the world. At his funeral, there were tributes from kings, prime ministers and presidents, including President Barack Obama of the U.S.

What a great honour it was to have met him, known him and learned so much from him. What an experience it was to have been personally advised by him along with the heads of states that sought his leadership, coaching and mentoring. As an exceptional leader, he could relate with people regardless of their race, culture, religion, political, or socio–economic status. His tactful and diplomatic ways inspired the famous and unknown, religious and secular, revolutionaries and conformists. He never hesitated to stand up for others and to speak up on controversial matters.

About three months after his passing, the Israeli government honoured him for his "ongoing contribution to the Jewish state." Israel's Tourism Minister, Uzi Landau, presented the Knesset Christian Allies Caucus and World Jewish Congress award to Dr. Munroe's son, Myles Munroe Jr., and daughter, Charisa Munroe, in a spectacular event held in Jerusalem. At the ceremony, Josh Reinstein, Director of the Christian Allies Caucus, said Dr. Munroe was courageous and had the "heart of a lion"—another attribute that made him an exceptional leader.

In his interview with the Christian Broadcasting Network (CBN), Reinstein additionally said, "Myles Monroe was a true Israeli hero. He stood up unabashedly in a lot of countries where it's not popular to talk on behalf of Israel and say that he loves Israel. He loves the people of Israel. He loves the God of Israel. He loves the Bible of Israel. For those reasons he left such an impact on the government of Israel, the State of Israel and its people."

Indeed, Dr. Munroe lived his life to the fullest. Through his business, ministry and personal way of being, he debunked many myths and unravelled many misconceptions of leadership. He led by example and heeded his own advice to die empty. Only true heroes are recognized for their greatness after death, and Dr. Munroe was one of those leaders.

There were times when I called his cell phone with the intention of leaving a voicemail only for him to answer. He gave me his undivided attention as if he was expecting the call all along. In fact, one of my phone calls woke him up from a nap which he must have squeezed into his busy schedule. However, he was calm, calculated and courteous; at no point did he ever make me feel intrusive.

From the numerous tributes that were shared either at his funeral or online, Dr. Munroe seemed to have had 'nine lives', which is probably why it took such a tragic plane crash to send him back to the Kingdom of God which he lived, preached and for which he eventually died.

One of the many prominent speakers at his home–going service was Ambassador Andrew Young, the former Mayor of Atlanta, a former U.S. ambassador, a civil rights advocate and close associate of the late Dr.

Martin Luther King Jr. He lauded Dr. Munroe as "a great leader, who, much like Dr. Martin Luther King Jr., died fulfilling their purpose, lifting up the downtrodden, clothing the naked, feeding the hungry and following the commands of God to lead others to freedom and opportunity never before experienced or even thought possible."

There is likely nothing that I can share about Dr. Munroe that cannot be found in his books, articles or videos. But something I feel compelled to share was the farewell advice he gave to me when leaving the Bahamas. He said, "Alex, you have it in you. You are pregnant with a vision that is larger than you. It is time to give birth. And when you do, remember these three things to beware of: glory, gold and girls."

He went on to explain how glory awaits those who live a life of purpose, how the popularity and prosperity which some people seek and die for notoriously are only worthy and sustainable if received as a result of the pursuit of purpose. In line with biblical teachings, he strongly advised that, while glory and fame should never be motivators of leadership, people are often attracted to leadership. "Glory is for God" he exclaimed repeatedly. He said fame should never be the focus, but in the humble belief of self as a source of inspiration to others.

As for gold, Dr. Munroe said that when we discover our purpose in life and give up everything for it, riches will come. But money must never be our motivator for leadership and should be managed effectively to fulfill the purpose and advance the vision. We must ensure that the prosperity that is derived from the pursuit of purpose is used to sustain and expand the vision.

He strongly believed that leaders should work hard to make themselves comfortable, but never at the expense of their purpose and the people entrusted to them. Gold must be spent to advance a vision that is greater than the self, as well as to expand the Kingdom of God.

Lastly, girls indicated the greatest temptation a man of purpose is bound to face. He related that his best form of protection against temptations when travelling around the world was to travel with his wife. It is one thing to have integrity and quite another to be wise and cautious.

He advised me to do the same; to never take my spirituality for granted, to always protect my marriage, and constantly develop myself. He reminded me power always attract temptations and some renowned corporate, community, political and even religious leaders have been disgraced because of the age–old temptation of indecent exploits.

While he was explaining this, the biblical story of King David came to my mind. King David was a man whom the Bible says was after God's own heart and a king loved by many. David wrote the most beautiful praises and prayers in the Bible, but despite his outstanding spirituality, he still succumbed to the beauty of Bathsheba. King David committed adultery with Bathsheba, the wife of one of his army commanders, Uriah the Hittite. To hide his sin, David went as far as orchestrating the death of his friend, Uriah, and married Bathsheba afterwards.

Dr. Munroe felt so strongly about this that the last book he published before passing on was *The Power of Character in Leadership: How Values, Morals, Ethics and Principles Affect Leaders.*

MY TRIBUTE TO DR. MYLES MUNROE

Dearest mentor, your passing has heightened our passion to build on your legacy of purpose, our quest to ignite the leadership spirit in everyone all over the world, especially in the developing nations.

Thank you for joyfully and completely giving yourself to the world. Rest assured that, like you, we shall "rob the graveyard" of our talents too. We shall maximize our potential and inspire millions to discover and fulfill their life purpose. We are committed to living our lives to the fullest, just as you did.

I feel deeply honoured to have known you so well, and grateful to God for using you to instruct me in the true way of leadership and guiding me to teach many people the concept of maximum living and massive success. Many of us may be saddened by your short life, but we are grateful for your selfless donation.

Bravo for having fought such an excellent fight, for having finished the race, for keeping the faith, just as the Apostle Paul did. You've given so much to us and built a legacy that will live forever. You did not have the chance to write the foreword for this book as you once offered, but you did more than that: you inspired it.

This is why I offer it as a tribute to you.

In your own words, "We weren't born just to live a life and to die; we were born to accomplish something specifically. As a matter of fact, success is making it to the end of our purpose; that is success. Success is not just in existing; success is making it to the end of why you were born."

Indeed, my trainer, coach, mentor, friend and brother, you successfully made it to the end of your purpose and did so exemplarily without a scandal. Even more, you clearly passed it on and even wrote a book, *Passing It On*, to guide us in sharing your message to the world.

As you always reminded us, if a little boy from a poor family of eleven siblings in poverty–stricken Bain Town, Nassau, Bahamas could rise above his unfortunate circumstances to become an iconic leader like you, then anyone can. You said that you did not want your name on buildings, but rather that your legacy is reflected in the outstanding leadership of your mentees.

This is why it is a great honour to dedicate this book to you and your noble wife, Ruth–Ann.

Rest well soldier, rest well, until we meet again.

Section One

The Purpose of Exceptional Leadership

Successful organizations understand the
purpose and original intent of leadership.
They realize that people's innermost desire is to
discover and fulfil their individual purpose in life,
so they strive to create a place of work or worship
where people can maximize their skills and talents.

Chapter One

The Misconceptions of Leadership

What Leadership Isn't

> "In no other area of management education is the concept of myth as prevailing as in leadership."
> – Jeffery Pinto

Before we get into what leadership is all about, it is very important to clarify what it isn't.

It is beneficial to know where most people and organizations get it wrong with leadership and why many parts of the world struggle to understand the true essence of leadership. Identifying the most common misconceptions about leadership was the most fascinating part of my research for this book. It revealed what leadership isn't, why it usually fails and the root causes of ineffective leadership in governments, organizations, churches and other institutions.

A misconception is a conclusion that was derived based on inaccurate presumptions, incorrect information or faulty thinking. It is what people have come to believe because of popular notion, but yet not the original truth.

Going through these misconceptions one by one gave me many 'aha' moments. It helped me to better understand the reasons for leadership failures, which everyone complains about but only a few can really explain. As Leonardo Da Vinci, the fifteenth century iconic Italian painter and sculptor, once said, "The noblest pleasure is the joy of understanding." As you go through these common misconceptions of leadership one by one, examine your own understanding of leadership so that you can seize the opportunities to unlearn and relearn where necessary.

I sure did.

Over two decades of consulting and coaching diverse groups of people from all over the world on leadership and personal development taught me that most people are sincere about their leadership endeavours, but yet are unfortunate victims of our modern misconceptions. I also learned that people's progress is hindered, not often by what they don't know, but more so by what they think they know.

While there may be some elements of truth in these misconceptions, they are definitely insignificant enough to be considered part of the leadership phenomenon. Unfortunately, an increasing number of those in positions of authority are failing in leadership because of these misconceptions.

By the time I sifted through the tons of research materials on leadership, I discovered a lot of information that directly or indirectly created these misconceptions. Some of these misconceptions may either be eye–opening to you or mere confirmations of what you already knew. Regardless, they are the primary reasons why leaders fail in governments and organizations around the world. As you go through them one by one, put more focus on yourself rather than on other victims of these misconceptions. Consider these revelations more as opportunities for self–discovery and self–awareness.

1. MISCONCEPTION OF POSITION

"The key to successful leadership is influence, not authority." (Ken Blanchard)

There is a prevailing misconception that leadership is about the position because leadership is often associated with job titles. This misunderstanding has deceived more people than all the other misconceptions combined. It has created the illusion that once you attain a certain level of authority, you become a leader. This is untrue.

You may become the head of a department, but not necessarily the leader in that department. The leader is the one who serves and sacrifices the most for a worthy cause. And if that is not you, you are not the leader, but rather merely the person with the position of authority. Job titles and positions are not indicative of leadership, but rather demanding of it.

When an organization sends out a communiqué to announce the hiring of a new chief financial officer (CFO), it usually indicates that a new leader has been hired for the finance department. While there is an element of truth in this, it does not automatically translate to effective leadership.

A new "leader" may have been hired for that department, but the position does not make the incumbent a leader, neither do the responsibilities. While many people unfortunately confuse leadership with positions of authority, positions of authority do not automatically translate to leadership in action.

Being the governor of a state is a rank of authority, just like a high court judge. But until you begin to demonstrate the leadership capabilities of informing, influencing and inspiring others, you are not a leader, but merely a person in the role of authority. No one has the right to claim the title of a leader. It is conferred informally by the beneficiaries of your hard work and sacrifice and by the consistent exceptionalism of your character and service.

Most job promotions, I discovered, are often based on education, experience and exposure rather than on the leadership abilities to effectively inform, influence and inspire others to achieve greater heights. Despite the value of education, experience and exposure, if that new CFO is unable to effectively inform, influence and inspire the people in his department, then that organization has merely hired just another employee. Andrew Carnegie and Henry Ford had no formal education, but because of their remarkable leadership capabilities, history classifies them as exceptional leaders of modern industrialization.

A cultural change is necessary for correcting this misconception in your organization. It requires a paradigm shift in the mindset of everyone in the institution, especially those who consider themselves as leaders because they simply hold positions of authority.

When governments and organizations consult with me on this topic, I work with them to build a corporate strategy that will inspire every employee to maximize their potential, regardless of their job title. The objective is to create a workplace where employees can best apply their talents and skills both inside and outside the organization.

Since titles and positions are important to organizational structure, communiqués about new positions should clearly indicate the role that is being filled. Corporate memos should emphasize how the leadership capabilities of the appointee or incumbent were instrumental in her successful promotion.

When an organization announces the hiring of a new "leader" instead of indicating the position, they would be subtly communicating to other employees that leadership is a title. They would be telling everyone else that the only person who is paid to lead is the person who was hired for it; everyone else must follow that person thereafter.

If you think that holding a position of authority automatically makes you a leader, you may never become one. Organizations that wish to advance their vision and mission should create a culture where employees can wilfully demonstrate their leadership capabilities, rather than a culture where they strive for positions of authority. This requires those in positions of authority to recognize leadership initiatives over productivity statistics, and regard social responsibilities as much as cost savings.

The future of organizations that promote employees based on outstanding leadership capabilities is more secure than that of those that promotes employees strictly based on education, experience and exposure.

People with outstanding leadership capabilities are always willing to learn, while those with education, experience and exposure often think they already know it all. Learning is a beneficial component of leadership; whereas an arrogant attitude is self–destructive in life and counterproductive in organizations. Nothing makes leadership more ineffective than this mindset.

Job titles and positions are so insignificant in the arena of leadership that many people are unaware of the positions which most iconic leaders held in their days. Do you know the job titles that were held by Mahatma Ghandi, Martin Luther King Jr. and Mother Teresa? What about Nelson Mandela before his imprisonment or before he became the president of South Africa?

These iconic leaders earned the right to be called leaders, not because they had positions of authority, but rather because they sacrificed everything for the purpose they so strongly believed in. Nothing else demonstrates exceptional leadership more than sacrifice.

In his book, titled *The Leader Without A Title*, Robin Sharma says, "Leadership is about knowing who you are, what you stand for, and then having the courage to be yourself—in every situation rather than only when it's convenient. It's about being real, consistent, and congruent so who you are on the inside is reflected by the way you perform on the outside." Whether you hold a position of authority or not, you should make every effort to become the best leader in the world.

2. MISCONCEPTION OF POPULARITY

"When leaders choose to make themselves bidders at an auction of popularity, their talents, in the construction of the state, (or whatsoever) will be of no service." (Edmund Burke)

There is a prevailing misconception that leadership is grounded in popularity because leaders are often more popular than others. This misconception often brings out the worst in those who strongly desire popularity and fame. They think that becoming a leader will make them the boss, the one with the answer to every question, the one in the forefront of every matter.

Without a question, everyone has a desire to feel loved, respected and appreciated; however, some people unfortunately see leadership as a means to gratify this innate and burning desire for praise and recognition. It isn't.

If your main objective in life is to be popular, your talents will be wasted. You can't seek leadership and admiration at the same time. Leadership may often attract others, but their adulations often distract leaders. The desire for popularity will hinder your effectiveness as a leader. It will create a repelling demeanour around you that will deter others from associating with you. It will destroy your relationships and derail your goals and objectives.

In the words of Immanuel Kant, the seventeenth century German philosopher, "Seek not the favour of the multitude; it is seldom got by honest and lawful means. But seek the testimony of few; and number not voices, but weigh them."

While the decision to assume leadership may eventually result in popularity, it does not make you a leader. In fact, those in positions of authority who gain fame unfortunately do so for notoriety rather than for nobility. The sadistic thirst that people have for bad news these days makes the media to be more interested in the scandals of those in positions of authority than in their achievements. So the admiration that some people seek by assuming positions of authority is often attained at their own demise.

I discovered more often than not, those who seek a noble vision always outperform those who pursue position, popularity, prosperity and power. When you truly wish to make an impact, have an unquenchable desire to make a difference in the lives of others and are determined to advance humanity, you will care less about the flattery of others.

An example is Michael Bloomberg, a self-made billionaire that later became the Mayor of New York for three consecutive terms. With a fortune of $35.7 billion, Bloomberg is considered by *Forbes Magazine* as the tenth richest person in America and the thirteenth in the world.

Despite his solid position, global popularity, abounding prosperity, enormous power and the large population that he had influence over, he stepped down to campaign for, and won three times in a row, the elections for the Mayor of New York. Even though he could have ran for the presidency, as most expected, he had a vision for the city of New York, a vision bigger than his fame and fortune.

Bloomberg leveraged what he already had to assume a position that would enable him to make an even greater impact. His purpose was to make life easier for the population of New York. Generations from now may not fully remember the technological innovations that made Michael Bloomberg prosperous and powerful, but history will never forget his profound influence on the lives of people through his philanthropic initiatives.

It is a wonderful thing to leave a mark on your employees, clients and shareholders. But it is an even greater goal to shape and form the lives of ordinary citizens, those who you may never meet, those whom you will benefit nothing from. A poll that was carried out by the *New York Times* in 2013 reported exceptional feedback regarding Bloomberg's policies.

The poll indicated high satisfaction rates for his initiatives, including his prohibition of smoking inside restaurants and bars, requirement that fast-food chains post calorie counts on menus; his mandate that restaurants display the letter grades given to them by the city; the pedestrian plazas he ordered installed around the city; the bike lanes he had constructed; the bike-sharing program he created. What an example of exceptional leadership for other political leaders.

The *New York Times* went on to say New Yorkers, who pride themselves on their fiercely independent style, have come to respect, and even like, Bloomberg's brand of elbows-out interventionism in their lives. One accountant from Queens, Marvin Gruza, praised Bloomberg, "Look at the ground. When you walk into the city it's a different city. You have bike lanes. Yes, construction and change is painful, but people will look back in ten or fifteen years and say we're glad he made us do it."

What will people say in ten or fifteen years from now about you as a leader? That they are glad you made them accomplish something?

In the sector of political leadership, I discovered that those who were often popular for their entrepreneurial achievements and community services before seeking public office outperformed those who assumed positions of authority without having achieved excellence in their prior endeavours.

This makes exceptional personal leadership a prerequisite for those who wish to run for public office. Anyone who seeks leadership because of a burning desire for position, popularity, prosperity, population and power is bound to be an ineffective leader, if not a dictator altogether.

Bloomberg did not serve as the 108th Mayor of New York City for three consecutive terms because of his quest for a place of authority. On the contrary, he wanted to serve, to make a difference, to impact the lives of those he may never meet and for generations to come.

Some notable acts of leadership that he demonstrated include his decline of salary from the city in an effort to reduce spending; his decision to maintain a public listing in the New York City phone directory, and to not live in Gracie Mansion, the official mayoral residence, but instead at his own home on the Upper East Side of Manhattan.

His exemplary leadership was furthermore illustrated by his refusal to use public funds, but rather spent $73 million of his own money on his campaign. Although his billionaire status may have given him an advantage, but there can be no doubt that his leadership spirit was ablaze and his motives were honourable. What about you? What are the sacrifices that you are willing to make in order to fulfil your purpose in life and advance a vision that will be a blessing for generations to come?

Those who pursue popularity at the expense of leadership will, sooner or later, find themselves on the opposite end of spirituality. It is a pursuit that will eventually lead to downfall.

Many people desire positions of authority for the sake of popularity out of ignorance and selfish motives. Bill Gates, Mark Zuckerberg and Oprah Winfrey were not seeking a popular admiration when they made tremendous sacrifices for their respective visions. Their passion and persistence gave birth to their successes. Only then did they become famous.

Are you focused on the fulfillment of your purpose in life and the execution of your vision or are you one of those who are pursuing position, popularity, prosperity, population and power at the expense of integrity? This is a question that people in positions of authority should ask themselves every day.

Rosa Parks was unknown until she suddenly sacrificed her own safety and assumed leadership by confronting the unjust law requiring "people of colour" to give up their seats on public transportation. Neither she nor anyone else at the time would have imagined the profound influence she was to have in this world by her courage. Yet she is renowned for her leadership and her witness to the rights of others.

Leadership is the act of standing up for justice despite the consequences. No one knew Parks' job title. She was an unknown woman. Yet, Bill Clinton articulated well the mark of her leadership, "The world knows of Rosa Parks because of a single, simple act of dignity and courage that struck a lethal blow to the foundations of legal bigotry."

Parks' act of leadership earned her the level of popularity that will live beyond our own time. Out of obscurity, her fight for justice earned her titles such as the "First Lady of Civil Rights" and the "Mother of Freedom Movement." When she passed away in 2005, she became the first woman and second non–U.S. government official to lie in honour at the Capitol Rotunda, a place reserved for ceremonial events and the lying in state of honoured people. Parks' sacrifice earned her a place among the iconic leaders of our time.

Moreover, on that fateful day, Parks discovered her purpose in life and its alignment with a vision that would benefit humanity. Hers was a vision that people such as Mahatma Ghandi and Martin Luther King Jr. were already advancing. Like them, she chose to ignite her leadership spirit without hesitation.

You can too.

There were many women and men who experienced the same oppression as Parks. Yet they yielded in the face of opposition and oppression. Few ascended the heights of leadership while Parks, and so many others, committed themselves to a vision despite the potential of being tortured, imprisoned and even killed.

In the words of Martin Luther King Jr., "The ultimate measure of a man is not where he stands in moments of comfort and convenience, but where he stands at times of challenge and controversy." Nothing tests your perseverance more than leadership.

3. MISCONCEPTION OF PROSPERITY

"Prosperity is only an instrument to be used, not a deity to be worshipped." (Calvin Coolidge)

There is a prevailing misconception that leadership breeds prosperity because leaders are perceived as rich. No other misconception about leadership breeds greed and corruption as much as this. When you assume a position of authority with this misunderstanding, theft is inevitable. Leadership is not about prosperity, but rather about philanthropy. It is about sacrifice and service, and giving. Until you are willing to sacrifice even the little that you have for the benefit of those who have less, you are not ready to lead.

As I considered the lives of Bill Gates, Mark Zuckerberg and Oprah Winfrey in my research, I discovered that they never sought out money. They simply summoned the courage to pursue their purpose in life and generated enough passion to eventually break through the financial challenges before attaining the billionaire status. Sadly, however, some people pursue positions of authority simply for the sake of prosperity. This is the mindset fostered by the greed and corruption that are also bankrupting global organizations and destroying many countries.

The abounding corruption in some developing nations is largely a result of this misconception. So, too, are the bankruptcies of Lehman Brothers, WorldCom and Enron. The number of senior government officials and executives found guilty of corruption, theft, money laundering and despicable breaches of trust increases daily basis because of this misconception. Deep within them is this erroneous notion that leadership offers wealth, whetting an unquenchable thirst for it.

Sacrifice is an essential virtue of leadership. Instead of using positions of authority to unscrupulously amass wealth, leadership requires you to sacrifice all that you have for the vision. The exceptional leaders the world adores sacrificed substantial portions of their personal and organizational fortune for noble causes. Much of their prosperity advances their vision rather than themselves. Nothing determines the impact of your vision more than the level of your sacrifice.

The prosperity that many billionaires enjoy today is simply a result of their sacrifices. Many of them insist that even though their leadership may have led to prosperity, a person should never ignite their leadership spirit simply for the sake of prosperity. If anything, prosperity should inspire leadership that gives back to humanity, such as The Giving Pledge initiative.

The Giving Pledge was started by Bill Gates and Warren Buffet many years ago with the objective of convincing billionaires to give 50% or more of their fortune to charity. By 2014, 127 billionaires had joined the initiative including CNN founder Ted Turner, Facebook's Mark Zuckerberg and New York Mayor Michael Bloomberg. Each of these leaders lived the essence of leadership by sharing the fruits of their labour through philanthropy.

Other leaders, such as the self-made billionaire from Nigeria, Tony Elumelu, recently pledged $100 million towards creating 10,000 entrepreneurs across Africa in the next ten years. His sharing with others exemplifies the essence of exceptional leadership.

On the other hand, nothing has hindered the progress of developing nations more than greedy and power-hungry leaders. Tragically, there are leaders known to seek public positions for the purpose of embezzling public funds. They seek to be praised and adored and yet do nothing for their electorates. As a result of their ineffective leadership and dictatorship, some nations have drastically regressed since gaining independence from their colonial masters, leaving their citizens in the unfortunate state of abject poverty and pain.

In the arena of religious leadership, we see instances of those in authority amassing wealth at the expense of their congregations. Jesus Christ reminds us that a true pastor goes without: "Foxes have dens and birds have nests, but the Son of Man has no place to lay his head." Yet some pastors have executive jets and multiples mansions while their congregations struggle to survive.

A recent study of the personal wealth of people in religious positions indicates nearly twenty of them valued up to three billion dollars. Tragically, many of these multibillionaire ministers are pastors of churches in what is considered the third world. If Jesus Christ had to borrow a donkey for the most triumphant entry ever made by man, how does one justify a pastor having three private jets?

There are also increasing instances of executives of non–profit organizations claiming the "right" to earn as much as their peers in banks and insurance companies, at the expense of donors who may be giving their "widow's mite." There is nothing about leadership that gives one power over another person. The only right a leader earns is the right to serve–strategically, sacrificially and successfully.

By no means am I suggesting leadership shouldn't lead to prosperity. On the contrary, a leader may and should experience great fruit from his work, yet prosperity shouldn't be the motivation for leadership. If your desire to be rich is stronger than your desire to serve, then you will compromise, and your leadership will be ineffective. Extravagance is simply weakness begging for wisdom. This is the paradigm shift that I speak of in this book.

Like popularity, there is a strong inclination of leaders to seek prosperity. Those who adopt leadership as a means to prosperity are impostors. They are deceivers motivated by greed. Those with these traits and are in positions of authority should be relieved of their roles and responsibilities for the sake of the vision. To be an exceptional leader requires you to focus unwaveringly on the pursuit of your purpose and advancement of the vision and not on the selfish quest for popularity, prosperity and power.

Like popularity, the prosperity gained in leadership is meant to enable you fulfill your purpose in life, to advance your vision and to expand the mission of your organization. Those who exploit popularity and plunder prosperity do so at their own peril.

Therefore, unbeknown to the members of The Giving Pledge, their philanthropic acts, which is sustained by their enormous prosperity and popularity, is a factual way of ensuring legacies for themselves and others. In the words of Winston Churchill, "We make a living by what we get, but we make a life by what we give." In other words, we don't give to get, but rather we give to live. Living without giving is death, even while living.

4. MISCONCEPTION OF POPULATION

"I start with the premise that the function of leadership is to produce more leaders, not more followers." (Ralph Nader)

Another prevailing misconception suggests people tend to follow leaders and that excellent leadership is determined by how many people follow you. Many people in positions of authority are becoming people pleasers because of the naïve notion that the numbers of people in your government, corporation, church, community or college are indicators of your leadership effectiveness.

It isn't.

In fact, leadership that seeks to gain followers is ineffective leadership. You may be the pastor of a mega church or CEO of a large organization and yet be an ineffective leader. To stand up for nothing because of your desire for more people is not leadership. Neither is leadership's main purpose to create excitement over nothing that really matters. This misconception has led more leaders to abandon their vision more than any other, for the fear of losing followership is turning them to followers rather than leaders.

According to John Caldwell Holt, an American educator, "Leaders are not as we are often led to think, people who go along with huge crowds following them. Leaders are people who go their own way without caring, or even looking to see, whether anyone is following them. Leadership qualities are not the qualities that enable people to attract followers, but those that enable them to do without them. They include, at the very least, courage, endurance, patience, humour, flexibility, resourcefulness, stubbornness, a keen sense of reality, and the ability to keep a cool and clear head, even when things are going badly. True leaders, in short, do not make people into followers, but into other leaders."

Leadership means to stand up for something significant, which, quite often, isn't always considered popular opinion. Therefore, the moment you water down your principles for the sake of population, you have given up the right to lead. On what premise do you start with? What do you consider the primary function of a leader? Are you easily swayed by public opinion? Do you put the concern of losing people over that of advancing the vision?

Leadership is driven by purpose and not by population, by vision and not out of a desire to please. It is more about the purity of the vision. It is about empowering people to achieve their purpose in life and not delay them from fulfilling it. Exceptional leaders inspire other people to discover their purpose and talents, and then help them develop the skills required to advance the vision. .

True leadership is not about growing the size of your followers, but rather by nurturing their true potential. Strikingly, the number of supporters does not demonstrate true leadership; in fact, few followers may actually indicate effective leadership. While it may be relevant to your vision, size is not a determinant of effectiveness.

The pastor of a church must be willing to send out members on church-planting missions when the church is getting too large. Having a mega-church where thousands of people travel across cities every week to attend your worship services may be a sign of ineffective leadership. It may mean that you are failing to "send out the twelve" and to "make disciples of all nations," in accordance with the vision of your CEO, Jesus Christ.

Some pastors shared with me their lack of confidence in their lieutenants. Some even confessed the fear they have of their deputies seceding if they are allowed to head branches of the organization. But allowing people to spend their time and money to travel across town because of your lack of confidence in others is an unnecessary risk. It is inefficient, ineffective and definitely not visionary.

Your primary role, as a leader, is to develop the leadership capabilities of those around you to the extent of trusting them to advance the vision when you leave. If you have too many people relying on you for too many things, your leadership is ineffective.

Regrettably, the perception that higher numbers indicate effective leadership creates ineffective leaders simply because they are too focused on pleasing those around them. Many people in positions of authority no longer stand for what is right, but rather for what is bright.

In the words of Lady Margaret Thatcher, the longest-serving British Prime Minister and the only woman to have held the office, "One of the great problems of our age is that we are governed by people who care more about feelings than they do about thoughts and ideas." It is ineffective leadership when you allow the feelings of people to trump the decisions that you must make.

Many corporations are beginning to understand that higher numbers may indicate ineffectiveness and inefficiency; hence, downsizing is now the buzzword in the corporate world. While unfortunate for those who lose their jobs, it is ineffective leadership that leads organizations to overstaff in the first place.

As a leader, you are meant to influence employees to maximize their talents and inspire them to develop their skills. Therefore, you shouldn't hire without first exploring within your organization. This is not about overworking your employees, but rather about influencing them to discover their untapped potential.

Downsizing may carry negative connotations, but it is a perfect opportunity for people to examine their lives, to discover their purpose, to become aware of untapped talents and skills and to pursue their longstanding dreams. Organizations are finally starting to understand this as I hope you are too.

If you must grow your followers, let it be those inspired by your vision. According to Mahatma Gandhi, "A small body of determined spirits fired by an unquenchable faith in their mission can alter the course of history." And they have.

5. MISCONCEPTION OF POWER

"If you want to test a man's character, give him power." (Abraham Lincoln)

There is a prevailing misconception that leadership is about power because of how powerful some leaders have become. While some leaders may have become powerful, leadership is not about power, but rather about empowering other people. It is a spiritual orientation of sacrifice and service, of humbling yourself so others are exalted. Like popularity and prosperity, power is a possibility when you ignite your leadership spirit, but it should not be the motive for igniting it in the first place.

The power that I refer to here is that of using authority to command and control a large number of people, as many governors, executives and pastors do. This power can be conferred upon you by others, acquired by force, garnered by virtue of social and religious status, or bequeathed by lineage through royalty. But regardless of how you possess this power, it does not automatically make you a leader.

You must consistently demonstrate the principles of exceptional leadership to be considered one. Having too much power in your hands does not make you a leader; on the contrary, it can easily make you a dictator.

The more power you possess, the likelihood of it possessing you in return. Take for example, Adolph Hitler of Germany, Idi Amin Dada of Uganda and Saddam Hussein of Iraq. These heads of states amassed so much power that they eventually became dictators. They abused the laws of their countries and committed despicable crimes against humanity. Their combined dictatorships resulted in the death of about 50 million people. Their power only exposed their weak character, their lack of substance and their hunger for authority.

While acquiring power doesn't make you a leader, a reasonable level of authority is required for exceptional leadership. But how much? Let your conscience guide you accordingly. But know that most of the people who amass power beyond reason often lack self-control; for it is only God who can possess power beyond our human understanding and yet not abuse it. To avoid the abuse of power, you must put a solid organizational structure in place to decentralize power.

To advance his vision for the City of New York, Michael Bloomberg required the power of a mayor. When his mission was completed, he did not allow the taste of political power derail his purpose in life, but rather, he gracefully returned back to head his booming Bloomberg organization.

The danger of amassing power is so serious that it is necessary for you to empower a group of people to collaborate with you. I discovered many non–profit organizations lacking in this area, particularly in churches. Some had no board of directors in place, while others had board members without experience or afraid to object to the decisions of their pastors. Dare to let people question your motives and directives without becoming defensive; only then will your leadership be effective.

Whether you are a professor, politician, pastor, parent, physician, you have no right whatsoever to dominate someone else. Your authority is to enable you to encourage others and not to frustrate them. When God gave dominion to humanity, it wasn't over each other but rather over the birds, animals and fish, over creeping things. Not human beings.

Your dominion should be over yourself and purpose in life, not over people, including your spouse and children. Nothing, absolutely nothing, destroys a man more than his desire to control another.

Make no mistake about it: we are all powerful beyond measure because God endowed us with power over our minds, and with dominion over our individual purpose on earth. But God didn't grant us power over each other. The fact that your position of authority gives you power over people and things does not make you a leader, but rather a servant for humanity.

Like position, popularity, and prosperity, power is a value–add that should be strictly used to expand your vision or it will be self–destructive and abused. Everyone possesses the power to make a difference in the lives of others, so the pursuit of any other form of power is a failure to recognize your great purpose in life.

Iconic leaders such as Martin Luther King Jr. and Mahatma Ghandi had no legal authority over anyone or situation. They were neither heirs to any kingdom nor were they government officials delegated with some form of judicial power. Yet they were powerful enough to inspire millions. We, too, have the ability to empower others and to inspire millions.

Abraham Lincoln and John Fitzgerald Kennedy used their power to demonstrate exceptional leadership. Both of them were former presidents of the United States of America. Each was assassinated for the morality of their leadership and their vision.

Before his assassination in 1865, Lincoln led the United States through the Civil War and its greatest moral, constitutional and political crisis. His courage preserved the Union, abolished slavery, strengthened federal government and modernized the economy.

Kennedy, before his assassination in 1963, orchestrated several negotiations that prevented a nuclear war with the Soviet Union, initiated the vision of Project Apollo that eventually placed man on the moon and laid the foundation for the Civil Rights Act in 1964, furthering Lincoln's vision.

According to Kennedy, "The denial of constitutional rights to some of our fellow Americans on account of race—at the ballot box and elsewhere—disturbs the national conscience, and subjects us to the charge of world opinion that our democracy is not equal to the high promise of our heritage."

Another remarkable example of political power used to steer the moral compass of a nation for the benefit of humanity is the Truth and Reconciliation Commission in South Africa by President Nelson Mandela. After unjustly spending twenty-seven years in prison for speaking against apartheid, Mandela was released and eventually became the first black African president of the country.

To calm the racial tension and mitigate the violence that was bound to erupt for the sake of vengeance, this commission was tasked to bring about forgiveness and reconciliation between both races for the despicable acts of apartheid and racism.

Despite this ground-breaking example, there were limited instances in developing nations where legal power was used to influence national progress. The abuse of power was rampant due to ineffective checks and balances and outright corruption. We've seen instances of citizens being forced to comply with directives against their personal beliefs or even against the law, as well as people in positions of authority obtaining resources and information by force.

Africa is the richest continent on the planet in terms of natural resources because of its large quantity of petroleum, gold, iron, diamond, salt, copper, silver, cobalt, bauxite, uranium and many other resources. However, based on the Gross Domestic Product (GDP) of most of the countries in Africa, it is also considered the poorest continent.

The obvious reason is the mismanagement of resources, which is a result of ineffective leadership and political dictatorship. Due to their burning desire for power, some presidents are in their fortieth year of dictatorship, while others passed away still with a grip on power through their offspring.

Dictatorship is a direct outcome of the abuse of power. Far from the essence of leadership, this is a subtle form of terrorism that is perpetuated by those who hold positions of authority in governments, corporations, churches or other forms of institution. Despite the purported progress of civilization, the number of national dictators in the world should amaze anyone.

The instances of the abuse of power in both developed and developing nations are appalling. Due to these misconceptions of leadership, visions that could have benefitted humanity are constantly derailed, dismissed or discarded.

The type of power indicated here is not something to aspire for, but rather something to inspire others with. If you think you need this power to be more effective in your leadership, then you have yet to understand the essence of it all.

Leadership is about influence, regardless of your position, popularity, prosperity, population or power. Leadership can only be demonstrated when power is not exerted. John Quincy Adams articulates this well: "If your actions inspire others to dream more, learn more, do more and become more, you are a leader."

THE FINAL ANALYSIS

Gathering these five misconceptions of leadership was revealing. It was obvious that we have the natural tendency to desire position, popularity, prosperity, population and power, and that a high level of self-awareness is required to manage this natural tendency.

To become an exceptional leader requires us to be consistently aware of these natural tendencies, to maintain absolute focus on our vision and be determined to fulfill our respective purpose in life. According to Abraham Maslow, "If you plan on being anything less than you are capable of being, you will be unhappy for the rest of your life."

Leadership is not about position, popularity, prosperity, population or power. It is about the purpose and the vision, the execution of a series of initiatives to make a difference in the world. Even though we will not be elaborating on them, other misconceptions include prestige, politics, profit, policies, processes and procedures.

Like the five misconceptions we elaborated on in this chapter, these are associated with leadership, but not indicative of effective leadership. While they may be instrumental in the grand scheme of things, they are by no means indicative of your effectiveness as a leader.

Another major misconception of leadership is to connect it to your personality. Your personality may be beneficial to sustain your leadership, but leadership is not about your personality. There are many people in positions of authority that have great personalities, but are ineffective in leadership. They generated a lot of buzz around their vision, but the vision neither advanced, nor developed the people associated with it. They had deep knowledge, vast experience and unparalleled exposure, but yet were remarkably ineffective in leadership.

Popular traits like charisma, eloquence and tact definitely enable people to be more effective in leadership. But they don't define exceptional leaders. According to Peter Drucker, "Leadership is not magnetic personality–that can just as well be a glib tongue. It is not 'making friends and influencing people'–that is flattery. Leadership is lifting a person's vision to higher sights, the raising of a person's performance to a higher standard, the building of a personality beyond its normal limitations."

Your challenge now is to question the motive of your leadership to see if it is influenced by any of these misconceptions. It is to identify what you may have to unlearn and relearn about leadership, while embracing what you must learn anew. It is to put into immediate practice the very essence of leadership. It is to examine yourself, provoke your own thoughts and question your own motives. It is to determine how much more you have to develop yourself before igniting your leadership spirit.

In the words of Isaac Newton, "A man may imagine things that are false, but he can only understand things that are true, for if the things be false, the apprehension of them is not an understanding." I list these vices of leadership to liberate you from the undue pressure that many people in positions of authority experience.

Now that you know, you are free to lead. Your journey en route to exceptional leadership has just begun.

Chapter Two

The Essence of Leadership

Original Purpose Of Leadership

"In a time of universal deceit, telling
the truth is a revolutionary act."
– George Orwell

Everything that is meaningful to man often falls under the category of life, leadership and love.

While this book mainly focuses on leadership, it is also about the essence of life and the meaning of love. These three facets of human existence are related, for your life can only be fulfilled when you express love and demonstrate leadership. And yet, myths and misconceptions have made life, leadership and love to become so complex that many people are unaware of their true meaning.

Some people go through life without knowing their purpose in it, they fall in love without knowing the meaning of love and they assume positions of authority with insufficient knowledge about the essence of leadership. Not even a good spirit, humble heart and willingness to learn can make up for the misfortune of doing something without knowing why. As Martin Luther King Jr. put it, "Nothing in the world is more dangerous than sincere ignorance and conscientious stupidity."

This common misunderstanding that was created by popular myths and prevailing misconceptions about these three facets of human existence are the reasons why the rates of divorce, suicide, murder, war and other form of atrocities are increasing in the world. Bankruptcies of organizations, moral decadence, economic downturn, disunity among churches and the breakup of homes are some of the consequences of not knowing the essence of life, leadership and love.

Most schools teach nothing about life, leadership and love and yet expect students to thrive in societies upon graduation. How unfortunate it is that some school boards spend millions of dollars to develop complicated and even unnatural sex education curriculum, and yet teach nothing about the fundamentals of love.

What is the original purpose and essence of leadership? How do we demonstrate leadership in our daily lives? What are the most important decisions of leadership? Are leaders born or made? Can leadership abilities be developed or are they innate? Is leadership and management the same thing?

Simply put, leadership is a moral compass that measures the depth of your vision for humanity. It is a measurement of how far you are willing to go for your purpose in life, for what is right, just, fair and honourable. It is a series of initiatives on your part that indicate your unquenchable passion for life and love, the amount of sacrifice you are willing to make for others to maximize their potential.

Leadership is to sacrificially and strategically champion a worthy cause that will benefit humanity for generations to come. In the words of Winston Churchill, "What is the use of living, if it be not to strive for noble causes and to make this muddled world a better place for those who will live in it after we are gone?"

Contrary to popular belief, leadership cannot be bad; it is either effective or ineffective. What is usually noted as bad leadership is, in fact, dictatorship. The very essence of leadership is a noble cause, positive energy, forward thinking, strategic advancement and progressive change. It is the demonstration of commitment, compassion, consideration and cooperation.

If your way of being is not characterized by truth, grace, integrity, hospitality, gentleness, harmony and unconditional love, it is not leadership. Leadership is not an act, but an art, for it demands the originality of an artist and it requires the level of imagination that can produce a masterpiece.

A dictator uses positions of authority to obstruct justice, foster racism, oppose the truth and oppress others. This is not so for those in positions of authority who are making every effort to the best of their abilities. They may be ineffective, but not bad. What is ineffective can become effective again, and what is damaged can be repaired. What is inferior, defective and deficient, we may even be able to enhance and develop.

Due to the commanding nature of dictators, they do not relate with people and situations. They demand and command, and dictate and direct. With no compassion or communication, they use force to make things happen rather than influence. Meanwhile, relationship is a critical part of leadership, for leaders are expected to relate to people and situation, to communicate with others and be compassionate, even with those who differ in opinions and beliefs.

Relationship is what happens when two or more people are able to effectively communicate and connect with each other, which is what exceptional leaders are known for. It is the ability to relate and associate with other people without prejudice. In the words of Theodore Roosevelt, "The most important single ingredient in the formula of success is to know how to get along with people."

Based on this philosophy, there are three Facets of Leadership: Effective Leadership, Ineffective Leadership and Dictatorship. Dictators are neither effective nor ineffective in leadership. They are not leaders at all. The difference between an effective and ineffective leader is a person's level of competence. But at least, both of them make every effort to be exceptional in leadership, to advance their respective vision, goals and objectives.

A dictator, on the other hand, thinks he knows it all and is unwilling to unlearn or relearn anything. With such arrogance, dictators are not fit to lead. Dictatorship is not a form of leadership but rather the absence of it.

Leadership is not a policy that can be revoked, a principle that can be disregarded or a plan that may fail. It is simply what is ignited within a person when he eventually discovers his purpose in life and makes an unwavering commitment to fulfill it, while enabling others to discover and fulfill their purpose as well.

Those in positions of authority who are neither doing this effectively nor willing to learn how to, should be relieved of their duties, as a measure to mitigate negative impact to their organizations. Exceptional leaders only postpone what they are willing to die left undone.

Leadership is the tireless pursuit of wisdom. He who thinks he knows it all, therefore, is not fit to lead, for leadership is learning and learning is leadership. In the words of John F. Kennedy, "Leadership and learning are indispensable to each other."

Leadership comes from a pure spirit ignited in people whose burning desire for positive energy and progressive change can no longer be contained. Anyone with a spirit other than that which illuminates the world for others is not a leader. He may demonstrate traits that effective leaders are known for, but if his vision is morally reprehensible, then he is a dictator, such as Adolph Hitler.

Considering the unfortunate scars which Hitler left on humanity due to his strong desire for supremacy, he was definitely not a leader. His political and religious views were fanatical and resulted in the death of millions of people. There was nothing moral, just or right about his quest for power.

Leadership is born out of a burning desire to do what is just. Even though it may go against popular opinion, leadership must be righteous and in perfect harmony with natural laws. Opinions may differ because of race, ethnicity, religion, gender, sexual orientation and socio-economic status, but natural laws are universal. If your vision is destructive rather than constructive, it is not leadership. Anyone who is committed to serve and protect, to foster harmony and tranquillity, while also making every effort to be creative, is a leader.

This is why Rosa Parks' blunt refusal to obey an unjust law is exemplary of exceptional leadership. So are the renowned initiatives that make history applaud leaders such as Frederick Douglass, Abraham

Lincoln, Mahatma Ghandi, Martin Luther King, John F. Kennedy, Mother Teresa and Nelson Mandela.

As Jim Rohm puts it, "All good men and women must take responsibility to create legacies that will take the next generation to a level we could only imagine." Parks' defiance may have been perceived by some as strictly beneficial to African–Americans. However, her witness was beneficial to everyone in America and, indeed, around the world. This is the essence of leadership–a sacrificial move in support of a worthy cause.

A leadership spirit cannot be hired or fired, selected or elected. It cannot be appointed, awarded or assigned. It is a pure sacrificial decision to stand up even if others choose to sit down; to speak up even if others choose to be silent. Nothing disables a leadership spirit more than fear of reproach, ridicule and repercussion. This is why courage, confidence and compassion are critical to exceptional leadership.

By virtue of its purpose, leadership rocks the boat and confronts the norm; or else, it is followership.

For leadership to be pure and effective, it must be void of selfish and malicious intent. If your actions are not consistently focused on a sacred purpose, the fulfillment of a noble vision and not inspiring others to discover and fulfill their purpose in life, you have yet to ignite your leadership spirit.

Your role as a leader is to excite people about a vision and then inspire and influence them to discover their purpose in it. But first and foremost, you must embody the virtues that would make the vision attractive to others. People don't follow people. They follow examples, dreams and visions. To be a leader requires you to be an example, a dreamer and a visionary

You owe it to those attracted by your vision to inform them enough to become wiser, inspire them enough to dream bigger, challenge them enough to learn more, encourage them enough to do more, influence them enough to ignite their own leadership spirit. Only then are you qualified enough to be called a leader. Your main objectives as a leader is to enable the transformation of others into leadership, for only then are you able to advance your vision.

To become the leader that you desire others to be requires you to foster the principles that you desire others to foster. Being an example is the most effective way to ignite the leadership spirit in others. As John C. Maxwell puts it, "A leader is one who knows the way, goes the way, and shows the way."

The fact that organizations claim to have leadership teams in place does not mean that they have a leadership culture. A group of people with positions of authority may be classified as a leadership team; however, their leadership is ineffective if the people in their organization, government, church or school would do nothing more than the bare minimum.

Leadership is about getting other people excited about a vision that would benefit humanity, and then empowering them to discover their individual purpose in it. If those in positions of authority cannot empower and energize their teams to be and do more for themselves and others, their leadership is ineffective. They are merely a subsection of employees who are educated enough to convince their organizations to pay them a lot more money for not doing what they are expected to do.

ORIGINAL PURPOSE OF LEADERSHIP

"The greatest leader is the greatest servant, the one most dedicated to meeting the needs out there in a hurting world full of needs." (James C. Hunter)

The purpose of leadership, which is also the original intent, is to be of service to humanity and not necessarily to lead people. When Adam, who is believed to be the first human according to the Bible, was placed in the Garden of Eden, God's instruction to him was, "Be fruitful and increase in number; fill the earth and subdue it. Rule over the fish in the sea and the birds in the sky and over every living creature that moves on the ground." Not over each other.

Simply put, the purpose of leadership is to serve. The Bible says "The Lord God took the man and put him in the Garden of Eden to work it and take care of it." Essentially, God called Adam into leadership. Adam was asked to lead the vision and care for everything else in order to ensure continuity. The original purpose of leadership, therefore, is to serve. It is to champion a worthy cause for humanity, which may or may not benefit us directly.

Over time, the original purpose of leadership has been overshadowed by the pursuit of positions, quest for popularity, desire for prosperity, hunger for followers and thirst for power. Nowhere in the original intent were these ever considered as part of leadership.

Despite His deity, Jesus Christ said, "The Son of Man did not come to be served, but to serve, and to give His life as a ransom for many." In essence, the original purpose of leadership is strictly to serve, to inspire others, and to make a difference, even if it ends up costing your life. This is what the iconic leaders we adore today did.

Successful organizations understand the purpose and original intent of leadership. They realize people's innermost desire is to discover and fulfil their individual purpose in life, so they strive to create a place of work or worship where people can maximize their skills and talents. They develop policies, procedures and processes with this in mind. This is a strategic approach to exceptional leadership, when those in positions of authority are committed to the continuous development of others for a greater good.

Since the original purpose of leadership is to serve, the concept of servant–leadership is a tautology, for servants are leaders and leaders are servants. Mustafa Kemal Atatürk, who is credited to be the founder of the Republic of Turkey, said it best: "I will lead my people by the hand along the road until their feet are sure and they know the way. Then they may choose for themselves and rule themselves. Then my work will be done."

In other words, the purpose of leadership is to uphold a vision so high that others are bound to discover their purpose in it. It is to inform, inspire and influence people to become champions of their individual destiny. To demonstrate exceptional leadership requires you to be a model.

People flourish when their organizations give them the opportunity to demonstrate their natural talents and develop related skills. In cultures such as these, loyalty, honesty, trust, teamwork and other attributes that enable success are rampant. This is because nothing brings out the best in people more than the sense of purpose more than a passion to outlive life.

Everyone has the capacity to inspire others to greater heights, but the few that choose to do so consistently are those who have ignited their individual leadership spirit and earned the right to be called leaders.

Upon defeating the Ottoman Empire in World War I, Atatürk successfully led the Turkish National Movement in the Turkish War of Independence. He embarked on political, economic and cultural reforms that transformed the former Ottoman Empire into a modern and secular nation–state.

It was under his leadership that thousands of new schools were built, primary education was made free and compulsory, women were given equal civil and political rights, and the burden of taxation on peasants was reduced. This is the purpose of leadership, to be committed to a noble cause, a worthy vision.

Until you make the ultimate decision to embark on the pursuit of purpose, your leadership spirit will be dormant. Your leadership spirit will have no aim, plan, and desire. It will remain inactive in the face of opportunity and withdraw in the face of challenge.

A leader is someone who refutes the impossible by his actions. Leaders never fail. Not even when they fall short. They get up too fast for failure to stick.

You may hold a position of authority and even be popular, prosperous and powerful, but unable to demonstrate leadership capabilities until you are willing to refute the impossible. You will be distracted by everything and procrastinate about the things that matter. Even when you work harder than everyone else, you will achieve nothing significant until your leadership spirit is ignited by purpose.

FOUNDATION OF LEADERSHIP

"Trapped in every follower is a hidden leader." (Dr. Myles Munroe)

The question of whether leaders are born or made has unfortunately created different schools of thought. We see very educated people demonstrating exceptional leadership abilities and conclude that leaders are made. We then encounter uneducated people demonstrating exceptional leadership capabilities and conclude that leaders are born. The mere question as to whether leaders are born or made is a misconception, for it implies that leadership is either endowed or bestowed.

At the time of Parks, access to education was limited for her and millions of African–Americans as a result of racial discrimination. African–American students were forced to walk to school, while the City of Pine Level, where she resided, provided bus transportation and a new school building for white students. She was taught to read by her mother at a young age and attended a segregated, one–room school that lacked adequate school supplies as basic as classroom desks. The opportunities for her to learn about leadership were not only limited, but intentionally stifled.

At the age of 16, Parks left school to care for both her sick grandmother and mother and never returned school until her husband enabled her to earn her high school certificate at the age of 19. Yet, she is ranked among the most exceptional leaders that America ever produced. So too are entrepreneurs such as Bill Gates, Mark Zuckerberg and the late Steve Jobs, all of whom dropped out of university to pursue their dreams and made billions of dollars doing so.

In fact, the world is full of exceptional leaders who are educated and exceptional leaders who are uneducated. The basis of their leadership abilities may be birth, but the basis of their exceptionalism is their sacrificial dedication to serve and not necessarily a formal education or training program.

So what is the final analysis? Are leaders born or made? If either, why are Parks, who was barely educated, and Martin Luther King Jr., who completed his Ph.D., both ranked among the greatest leaders that America ever produced? How come Bill Gates who has no university degree and Warren Buffet who has an advanced degree from Columbia University are both billionaires and irrefutable geniuses in leadership and entrepreneurship?

The truth of the matter is that everyone is endowed with the leadership capabilities that they require to achieve their life purpose. However, it is up to them to develop the related characteristics that will enable them to become exceptional leaders.

Parks may not have had a university degree, but she had the leadership traits inside her all along; they simply were unleashed on that fateful day. Indeed, trapped in her all along was the Parks that she eventually introduced to the world through a single act of courage.

Like a fly that is trapped in a capped bottle, the leadership capabilities in many people beg to be unleashed for the betterment of humanity. Is this you? Have you assumed the leadership of the purpose you were created for? When will you make the decision to stand up for a noble cause?

Everyone can lead in some way, shape or form. In fact, everyone was born to lead a purpose, a dream and a vision. You were born to unleash your talents to advance a vision that will benefit future generations.

If you are humble enough to subject yourself to learning, your confidence and capability will increase tremendously. This is the prerequisite for exceptional leadership–a humble desire to learn, grow and serve. The question should not be whether leaders are born or made, but rather how can each person's innate leadership spirit be ignited.

To be a leader you have to discover your purpose in life and the talents God gave you to fulfill it. You must become aware of how your purpose in life fits into a noble vision for humanity. Then you must identify and develop your talents and the related skills. Once you are ready, the opportunity will present itself as it did for Parks on that fateful day. If it doesn't, then create it for yourself.

Michael Jordan and Wayne Gretzky are two of the greatest athletes of our time. Their talents enabled them to attain the highest level of position, popularity, prosperity, population and power. Undoubtedly, both of them were born with natural athletic capabilities that were instrumental to their successes; however, they still had to develop the skills they required to become exceptional at their games. It is the same for leadership. What you have in you can only get you so far. To go further requires a robust plan to ensure consistent personal development.

Jordan and Gretzky may have been born with some innate leadership abilities, but they enhanced those traits and developed new ones in order to become exceptional. While some fellow athletes were unscrupulously taking performance–enhancing drugs to sustain their quest for position, popularity, prosperity, population (fans), and power, both Jordan and Gretzky were busy working on themselves. They were building momentum, strengthening their dedication and enhancing their devotion to excellence.

Gretzky once said that the highest compliment you could ever pay him was to say that he worked hard every day. What would you consider the highest compliment for you?

LEADERSHIP AND VISION

"One plants what future ages shall enjoy." (Statius Caecilius)

No misconception is more limiting than to confuse purpose with vision, and no vision is more unsustainable than one linked to no purpose. Contrary to popular belief, these are two distinctive concepts in life. Vision and purpose are related, but different; although both of them are instrumental to the degree of greatness that you will unveil in your lifetime.

Purpose is what you must fulfill in life, while vision is what it would look like to other people. Purpose is what you must live for, while vision is what you must be willing to die for. It is only when you embrace your purpose that a vision is born. Until then, you are merely dreaming.

In one of my speaking tours, I spoke 16 times in nine cities on three continents to a combined total of over 5,000 people in 21 days. I travelled across North America, Europe and Africa, and spoke to groups of corporate executives, entrepreneurs, government officials, religious congregations and youth. This is when it became evident to me that the world's foremost problem is not necessarily poverty or terrorism, nor wars, climate change or diseases like HIV and Ebola; rather it is simply the lack of knowledge.

It is the fact that too many people are roaming the world without knowing their purpose in life. Your leadership spirit can only be ignited when in the pursuit of your purpose in life, when you are so determined to empower other people to do the same too.

I am convinced that if people only knew the exact reason for their existence, and are inspired to fulfill it, they would be happy for the rest of their lives. They will always make every effort to refrain from the hate and havoc that the world is so full of today. Greatness is to know your purpose in life, have a vision for it and an unquenchable passion to fulfill it. It is one thing to know your purpose and quite another to have a vision.

Sadly, many people don't know their purpose in life. But even more unfortunate is that many of those who know their purpose in life are either doing nothing about it or running away from it as Prophet Jonah did in the biblical tale. It wasn't until a huge fish swallowed him up and brought him back to his purpose that he decided to pursue it with passion and determination. Must you wait to hit rock bottom before deciding to pursue yours?

Many people wake up every day for jobs they don't like and for salaries that undermine their value. Some may have discovered their purpose in life but yet have no vision for it. No other life is worth living than the one you were created for. If you are not living your dream, you are certainly asleep in someone else's dream. Nothing you have done or will ever do can make it impossible for you to unveil your greatness, if you are so determined. No one can hold you back, keep you down or take you out ... but you!

You were built for success and should waste no time in living life to the fullest. While we understand vision as having the ability to see, the vision that is referred to here is the vivid imagery of the end result of your purpose in life. First used in the 14th century, vision is the image of an idea, a thought, dream, concept or the eventual state of an object or desire that would bring you fulfillment.

Purpose is the exact reason you were created, while vision is how far you are willing to go when it is all said and done. Leadership is what happens between both of them–your purpose and vision. The effectiveness of leadership is based on how far you are able to advance your vision. Knowing your purpose is great, but until you craft a vision that is based on it, the process of leading is yet to begin.

A vision is a desirable enhancement to the current state of anything, which is in line with your purpose in life. It can only be advanced rather than achieved, dreamed about rather than brought about. Your role as a leader is to ensure that your vision is continually progressing and passionately impacting until you fulfill your purpose in life.

The vision of the School of Greatness is "A Renewed Mind For Everyone™." We do this through books, speaking engagements, coaching programs, training sessions, consulting services, social media, T.V. and Radio interviews, and a host of other mediums and methods. It is this vision and associated activities that defined our mission "To make people think deeply, act passionately and grow steadily™."

Vision is often misconstrued for mission, goals and objectives. However, objectives are tactical, goals are strategic. Objectives are primary and goals are visionary. It takes many objectives to achieve a goal and many goals to advance a vision.

Goals and objectives are flexible, and even the mission may be subject to change. But the vision is non-negotiable. In a soccer game, the vision of the team may be to be the best soccer team ever; however, to be that, the team must win the World Cup. They must achieve the goal of winning their games by scoring more goals during all their matches. While each position in the team has an objective, the mission of the team is to work well together in order to maximize the potential of its players, in support of the goal to win the World Cup, so they may advance the vision of being the best soccer team ever.

Goals, by virtue of their strategic nature, are achieved through leadership, while objectives, by virtue of their tactical nature, are achieved through management. Filling a vacant position in your organization is a mere objective—not a goal. The goal is to ensure that the organization has enough capacity to keep fulfilling a mission, which advances the vision of the organization.

Goals will not motivate you as much as the ultimate reason why you must achieve them; and that is the vision. It is the 'why' (vision) that reveals the 'how' (mission), which clarifies the 'what' (goals), which, in turn, indicates the 'when' (objectives). To live your life to the fullest requires you to grasp your importance to God and to the world. It requires you to embrace the magnitude of the purpose you were created for, the cross you must carry, the vision you must execute. This is exceptional leadership.

PERSONAL AND ORGANIZATIONAL VISION

"If you are working on something exciting that you really care about, you don't have to be pushed. The vision pulls you." (Steve Jobs)

What is your personal vision? What is the vision of your organization? How do your personal and corporate objectives connect? What are the goals and objectives to advance your vision? Is your vision clear to everyone else, as clear as those iconic leaders who we adore today?

Lack and pain are the incubators of purpose. Until you are deeply troubled by the lack of something that would be beneficial to humanity, you will not become pregnant with your purpose in life. You will not be able to give birth to a vision that would eventually create a legacy for you.

Martin Luther King Jr.'s purpose was to speak up for the civil rights of those considered minorities. But his vision was a truly United States of America that offered everyone equal opportunities, regardless of their race, gender, religion and other forms of diversity.

The 13-month boycott of the buses between 1955 and 1956 in Montgomery due to racial segregation at that time was only an objective for the civil rights movement to achieve one of the goals they were working on. Has the vision been fulfilled? No, because vision can only be advanced and no necessarily fulfilled in our lifetime. Is the vision progressing well? The historic election of President Barack Obama for two consecutive terms is a testimony to the progress of Martin Luther King Jr.'s vision.

Can the vision ever be accomplished? No, because there will always be people who harbour racial discrimination in the U.S. Will there always be room for improvement? Yes, and initiatives like the Affirmative Action in the U.S. and Employment Equity in Canada are some of the significant improvements over the years. These are notable successes to advance the vision.

Vision is a driver, and not a destination. The imagery of how perfect things can be in life is meant to keep us awake, determined, focused, purposeful and passionate until we leave a legacy for the next generation.

Before becoming the C.E.O. of Apple, Tim Cook described the vision of Apple in 2009, while serving as chief operating officer:

> We believe that we are on the face of the earth to make great products and that's not changing. We are constantly focusing on innovating. We believe in the simple not the complex. We believe that we need to own and control the primary technologies behind the products that we make, and participate only in markets where we can make a significant contribution. We believe in saying no to thousands of projects, so that we can really focus on the few that are truly important and meaningful to us. We believe in deep collaboration and cross-pollination of our groups, which allow us to innovate in a way that others cannot. And frankly, we don't settle for anything less than excellence in every group in the company, and we have the self-honesty to admit when we're wrong and the courage to change. And I think regardless of who is in what job those values are so embedded in this company that Apple will do extremely well.

Is anyone in your organization able to describe the vision of your organization with this much conviction, clarity and passion, whether in a position of authority or not? Can you? No wonder Apple Inc., which is already the world's largest company by market capitalization, hit a record intraday value of $700 billion in November 2014.

Indeed, if you are focused on your vision with this much passion and determination, willing to do whatever it takes to sustain your mission and achieve your goals and objectives, you will do even greater things. However, if you are overly focused on self, strictly on financial gains, on popularity, prosperity and power, your vision will be compromised and your leadership, contaminated.

Vision is a by-product of your imagination. You can't rise above your imagination, simply because it is infinite. Since vision can only be advanced and not necessarily achieved, set bigger goals simply because you can achieve even bigger ones. Keep in mind that vision without passion is dead; so is purpose without principle. They must go hand in hand or else you will be disabled.

Having and focusing on your vision is so important that God once said through the prophet Hosea that, "People perish for the lack of vision." Basically, being unaware of your purpose in life and not having a vision that would impact humanity is suicidal and detrimental to humanity.

LEADERSHIP AND MANAGEMENT

"Management is doing things right; leadership is doing the right things." (Peter Drucker)

Another prevailing misconception about leadership is the confusion between leadership and management. As already established, leadership champions a greater cause, a noble vision, an aim or objective for the benefit of humanity; while on the other hand, management is the effective command and control of efforts and resources. There must be a perfect balance between management skills and leadership capabilities in order for a vision to be advanced strategically and successfully.

Management is a critical aspect in the advancement of your vision. It is so critical that those with exceptional leadership capabilities will fall short of their objectives if they do not apply the techniques of management. Henri Fayol, one of the most influential contributors to modern concepts of management, indicated that it consists of these six functions: Forecasting, Planning, Organizing, Commanding, Coordinating and Controlling.

Based on these functions, you can forecast how many people you need to execute an objective. You can even plan the task, organize the flow of work, command the volume of production, coordinate their efforts and control the process. This is the essence of management.

Like leadership, management was never meant to be over people. Regardless of the situation, people reserve the right to exercise freewill, and to subject themselves to the self and the self only. The verb 'manage' derives from the Latin word, *manus*, which means to give a hand. The word later evolved into the English word management around the seventh century. Therefore, a manager was initially created to "give a hand" strictly with respect to available resources. He was not to lead people, but rather to focus on doing whatever it takes to get the job done. This may or may not include acts of leadership.

A manager of inventory may be exceptional in the role; however, if he is also responsible for other employees in the organization, then his leadership abilities must be developed or else he is bound to fail. He may be responsible to formulate policies, processes and procedures; however, if he is unable to influence and inspire other employees to adhere to them accordingly, his efforts are inutile.

Since everyone in an organization must report to someone else, then those in positions of authority must learn to balance their management skills with their leadership abilities. They must learn to be exceptional in leadership as much as in management, for leadership and management must go hand in hand for successful outcomes; or else, your vision will be stagnant.

Leadership and management are very distinctive responsibilities that complement each other to advance any vision. It is one thing to influence and inspire people to action, which is leadership, but quite another to direct resources effectively, which is management.

To successfully advance your vision, you need leadership abilities to inform, influence and inspire others and management skills to manage available resources. Efficiency is often a result of management, while effectiveness is often a result of leadership.

Your primary duty may be to ensure the resources of an organization are effectively allocated and efficiently maximized according to plan, but to be successful in this mission requires you to leverage your leadership capabilities to influence others to cooperate with you when preparing the budget and also collaborate with you to achieve it.

Thus, if you have not yet awakened your leadership spirit, you will not be successful in your primary duty as a manager. Organizations that hire strictly based on the ability to manage, without ensuring that incumbents have ignited their leadership spirit, do so at their own peril.

My research indicates that leadership is more about the vision, while management is more about the mission. Leadership is more about the overall goal, while management is more about the associated objectives. Leadership is more about the people, while management is more about the process. Leadership is sustained by contagious passion, while management is sustained by commanding procedures. Leadership often attracts people to the vision, while management often subtracts people from the vision. Leadership is more subjective, while management is more objective.

Leadership initiates, while management mitigates. Leadership inspires, while management informs. Leadership proposes, while management disposes. Leadership innovates, while management renovates. Leadership listens, while management speaks. Leadership focuses on the purpose, while management focuses on the planning. Leadership generates the excitement, while management accelerates the execution. In retrospect, leadership can only be effective when management is efficient.

Leadership and management complement each other and do not compete with each other. It is a misconception to say that the CEO is a leader while the CFO is a manager. They simply have different roles that may or may not be reflective of their levels of strength in both leadership and management.

THE POWER OF PARTNERSHIPS

"Coming together is a beginning; keeping together is progress; working together is success." (Henry Ford)

To better understand the crucial need of both leadership and management in the advancement of a vision, I examined the strengths of famous partners who executed historic goals and objectives in their lifetime; from the likes of Moses and his brother, Aaron, in the biblical times, to Bill Gates and Paul Allen. I also studied the respective strengths of the five co–founders of Facebook, Mark Zuckerberg, Eduardo Saverin, Andrew McCollum, Dustin Moskovitz and Chris Hughes.

As Vince Lombardi put it, "Individual commitment to a group effort–that is what makes a team work, a company work, a society work, a civilization work." These partnerships strongly exemplified the power of the critical pair; that is, leadership and management.

In most cases, we realized that the visionary who often possessed a higher degree of leadership abilities was usually more popular and prosperous in the partnership. However, he would not have been so successful without the other partner with the management skills. While Moses was often the one liaising with God to execute the vision of releasing the Israelites from bondage in Egypt, Aaron and his sister, Miriam, were responsible for the management of affairs on the ground.

Another historic business partnership I examined was the partnership of those behind McDonald's restaurant. Initially started in 1940 by Richard and Maurice McDonald, it was taken to greater heights in 1955 when businessman Ray Kroc joined the company as a franchisee.

Kroc realized that while the McDonald brothers were effective in managing the operations of the business, their desire was to only maintain a few restaurants, which was not visionary enough. The McDonald brothers were excellent managers but not exceptional leaders. So Kroc eventually purchased the company from them in 1961 for only $2.7 million and took it global.

Today, McDonald's Corporation is the world's largest chain of hamburger fast food restaurants, serving around 68 million customers daily in 119 countries across 35,000 outlets. The company's annual revenue in 2014 was $27.4 billion, with a profit of $4.5 billion. With 1.9 million employees, it is the world's second largest private employer, after Walmart.

Ray Kroc invested in the company because he was impressed by the management skills of the McDonald brothers. But with a vision as noble as he had, coupled with his remarkable leadership abilities, the company is now a global giant. This is what happens when leadership meets management and vice versa. The McDonald's brothers should have partnered with Ray Kroc; not sell off their dream to him completely. But then, that is a visionary idea as well.

It is a demonstration of exceptional leadership to know which of the critical pair your strength is, so that you may develop the other. The strengths and weaknesses of everyone, especially of those in positions of authority, fall under either leadership ability or management skills. What you must learn in order to fulfill your purpose in life falls under one or the other as well.

It is in your best interest to ensure that your associates have both leadership ability and management skills. Like Mark Zuckerberg, find your own Eduardo Saverin. Besides developing yourself in both areas, your utmost challenge as a leader, your task of all tasks, is to form a team of capable people with talents that complement each other and are all passionate about the vision.

Until you have a very effective team in place, you are yet to begin the process of leading. In the words of Theodore Roosevelt, "The best executive is the one who has sense enough to pick good men to do what he wants done and self–restraint enough to keep from meddling with them while they do it."

Leadership will uphold the vision in your mind, but it is management that will tell you how to get there and what to do to go further. If you are in a position of authority or wish to execute any vision, you must strive for both or else you are disabled.

Section Two

The Principles of Exceptional Leaders

Your character is a culmination of your habits.
To change your character, change your habits.
To change your habits, you must follow a set of
definite principles that were delicately put together
to influence your mindset and behaviour.

Chapter Three

The Seven Organic Laws of Leadership

The Prerequisite for Exceptional Leadership

> "Look deep into nature, and then you
> will understand everything better."
> – Albert Einstein

Can you imagine living in a country with no laws, where everyone is free to do what they want, when they want and how they want it done? What do you think would be the outcome of the universe if it were not governed by natural laws, or the output of an organization that had no rules and regulations?

With so many opinions, myths and misconceptions, this is the unfortunate state of leadership today. It is now left for people to decide what leadership is and how to demonstrate it. It is no wonder that many parts of the world remains underdeveloped. People assume positions of authority with no knowledge of the original laws that govern leadership.

The primary difference between human and natural laws is that while human laws change with time, natural laws does not succumb to time, not even to change itself. Contrary to the popular notion that change is constant, natural laws are not subject to change. Whichever way you look at it, regardless of your belief, culture, ethnicity and socio–economic status, the law of gravity is unchangeable. If you jump off the CN Tower without the gears to land safely, you will die.

The Seven Organic Laws of Leadership that I will unveil are based on the original purpose of leadership. They have been present from the beginning of time and will always remain. They are not affiliated with any religious, political or academic tradition, but must be adhered to by everyone who desires success in life, leadership and love.

They are based on years of deep psychological, physiological, spiritual and philosophical research transcending religious, cultural, racial and socio-economic backgrounds. These seven organic laws encompass the principles and characteristics of what is expected of exceptional leaders. They are exemplified in the lives of the leaders whom the world reveres today.

When these seven organic laws are adhered to, leadership is exceptional and exemplary. When they are breached, leadership becomes ineffective. When they are disregarded, leadership is replaced by dictatorship. These laws are so universal that they are the basis of every corporate, religious and governmental law, rule and regulation, which is not made by authoritarian and totalitarian regimes. They are so interconnected that breaching one could easily result to you breaching all of them. In the words of Cecil B. DeMille, "It is impossible to break laws. We can only break ourselves against the law."

1. THE LAW OF SPIRITUALITY

"Leadership is based on a spiritual quality; the power to inspire, the power to inspire others to follow." (Vince Lombardi)

By virtue of its original purpose, as extensively discussed in the first chapter, leadership is a spiritual concept. You must be possessed by a leadership spirit in order to be effective in it. To be spiritual is to be incorporeal or immaterial. Simply put, it is to do unto others as you would like them to do unto you. It is to consistently foster what the apostle Paul once classified as the Fruits of the Holy Spirit: love, joy, peace, patience, kindness, goodness, faithfulness, gentleness and self-control.

In the words of Albert Einstein, "It is clear that 'serving God' was equated with 'serving the living'. The best of people, especially the prophets and Jesus Christ, fought tirelessly for the spiritual."

Any attempt to lead any vision or champion any cause without fostering these Fruits of the Holy Spirit will quickly make your leadership ineffective before turning you into a dictator. Traits like authenticity, integrity, gentility, generosity, humility and hospitality, which distinguish the exceptional leaders we adore, are spiritually–based.

This is beyond whatever religion you practice or whatever your faith is. It is based on simple acts of loving and respecting yourself and others. In fact, nothing is more absurd than leadership without spirituality, when leadership at its best is the outcome of spirituality.

While the other laws of leadership in this book are instrumental to the effectiveness of your leadership, the Law of Spirituality is considered the most powerful of them all. Just like some laws in our judicial system are more powerful than others, this law carries the most weight.

If you breach the Law of Spirituality, you will be guilty of breaching the other six laws; for it is spirituality that will compel you to be sacrificial and to be of service to anyone else. Nothing is more spiritual than strategy, for the creation of the universe and the purpose of everything in it is one grounded in solid strategy.

Chaos is certain the instant that the Law of Spirituality is disregarded by those in positions of authority in corporations, churches, colleges or communities. It was the breach of this law that turned some people in positions of authority, like Adolph Hitler, Idi Amin Dada and Saddam Hussein, into tyrants and dictators. It was the lack of spirituality on the part of the executives that corrupted global conglomerates like WorldCom, Lehman Brothers and Enron. Whether you are religious or not, spirituality is a key to success.

The failure of leadership, which corrupts governments and corporations in the countries that arrogantly consider themselves the most advanced, is the result of breaching the Law of Spirituality. As Albert Einstein puts it, "A knowledge of the existence of something we cannot penetrate, of the manifestations of the profoundest reason and the most radiant beauty—It is this knowledge and this emotion that constitute the truly religious attitude; in this sense, and in this alone, I am a deeply religious man."

The craftiest initiative in the world today, is the systematic method by which spirituality is being eliminated in every system of government, schools and communities. Some countries still declare allegiance to God in their national anthems and pledges, yet they continue to enact laws which clearly instruct the schools, communities and government agencies to eradicate every form of belief in God. As Francois de La Rochefoucauld puts it, "Hypocrisy is the homage vice pays to virtue." If ineffective leadership is not curbed, it soon becomes dictatorship.

Moreover, the continual breach of this law is the cause for the astronomical rate of violence, murder and theft, the reason why we see an increase of divorce, addiction and suicide. In the words of Deepak Chopra, "Enlightened leadership is spiritual if we understand spirituality, not as some kind of religious dogma or ideology, but as the domain of awareness where we experience values like truth, goodness, beauty, love and compassion, and also intuition, creativity, insight and focused attention."

It is the Law of Spirituality that will compel you to love your neighbour as yourself. It is the Law of Spirituality that will compel you to stand up for what is right, just, fair and honourable. The biblical principles are all part of the Law of Spirituality. If you are not able or willing to uphold this Law of Spirituality, you are not fit to lead. No level of education, depth of experience or width of exposure qualifies you to lead more than The Law of Spirituality.

Leadership and love are inseparable. In fact, they are one and the same. In his open letter to the Corinthians, the apostle Paul writes, "Love is patient, love is kind. It does not envy, it does not boast, it is not proud. It does not dishonour others, it is not self–seeking, it is not easily angered, and it keeps no record of wrongs. Love does not delight in evil but rejoices with the truth. It always protects, always trusts, always hopes, and always perseveres. Love never fails."

This is the Law of Spirituality, the foundation upon which, exceptional leadership stands.

2. THE LAW OF SACRIFICE

"There is no moral authority like that of sacrifice." (Nadine Gordimer)

The ultimate price for leadership is sacrifice. It is your readiness to give up things that are most precious to you in support of the purpose that you were created for and the vision that you are blessed to lead. If you are not willing to give sacrificially, you are not ready to lead successfully. The first Law of Leadership, which is the Law of Spirituality, is meant to prepare you for this. Sacrifice is simply the surrender of something that is valuable for the sake of something that is invaluable. The ultimate sacrifice in life is life itself.

With the exception of a few, most iconic leaders gave up their lives for the vision they believed in. Jesus Christ was crucified for His vision to establish the Kingdom of God on earth. Abraham Lincoln was assassinated for his desire to make slavery unlawful. Mahatma Ghandi was assassinated for his profound belief in non–violence. John F. Kennedy and Martin Luther King Jr. were assassinated for their vision of a truly United States of America. Finally, Nelson Mandela sacrificed most of his life by choosing to languish in jail for the vision of a free and fair South Africa.

Sacrifice does not always lead to death. However it sure brings about excruciating pains essential to personal development. Leadership is the absolute resolve to put nothing else above the vision, not even your life or your relationship with others. When Mother Teresa left her home at the age of 18 to join the Sisters of

Loreto as a missionary, she never saw her family again. It was a sacrifice that she had to make to sustain the vision within her.

Nothing gives you the right to lead as much as the sacrifice you are willing to make, for it is what you are willing to give up that will make others to increase their support and dedication to your vision.

Sacrifice is more than just staying late at work every now and then and it is not about giving up what everyone else is ready to give up. According to Martin Luther King Jr., "Human progress is neither automatic nor inevitable. Every step toward the goal of justice requires sacrifice, suffering and struggle; the tireless exertions and passionate concern of dedicated individuals." Whatever sacrifice you are willing to make for your vision must be proportionate to the vision or it is preposterous.

The Law of Sacrifice requires you to give up all that you are and have for the fulfillment of your purpose in life, for the vision that you were born to advance. In fact, you must be willing to stretch yourself even further for those who are attracted to your vision. These are the top two sacrifices that will yield remarkable results for the communities you serve and would enable you sustainably advance your vision.

No research would have enabled me to understand the level of sacrifice that Martin Luther King Jr. made for his dream until I had the honour of spending some time with his daughter, the reverend Bernice King. She told me stories of how her father made tremendous sacrifices to advance his vision. And today, about 47 years after his death, some of those sacrifices are still being made in the family.

An extraordinary entrepreneur who made a great sacrifice is the thirty–year–old Elizabeth Holmes. She sacrificially dropped out of her sophomore year in the prestigious Stanford University to found the blood testing company Theranos in 2003. She did so with the money that she saved for college. Her vision was to create a substitute to the age–old and painful way of blood testing. And today, with a simple painless prick, her laboratories can quickly test a drop of blood at a fraction of the price and vial needed by commercial laboratories.

The Law of Sacrifice demands that you make significant sacrifices for those attracted to your vision. This sacrifice may come in the form of a pay cut on your part so that you may be able to afford the pay of your employees. It may also require you to put in extra personal time to train, coach and mentor those who are attracted to your vision.

The sacrifices you make for those you lead are what will bring out the best in them and ultimately generate returns and dividends for your organization. In the words of Napoleon Hill, "Great achievement is usually born of great sacrifice, and is never the result of selfishness."

Salaries and benefits, regardless of how steep, do not constitute sacrifice for an organization because they are the dues which must be paid to its employees. However, the quality of one–on–one time to develop your population is what counts the most. If you wish to become an exceptional leader, you must first identify the sacrifices that you must make.

This is why I applaud Dan Price, who, at the age of 19, founded Gravity Payments in 2004, with his brother, Lucas. Gravity Payments quickly grew from its small start–up roots to a company with over 100 employees, making it the largest payment processor in Washington State with clients located across the United States of America. In June 2010, Price was honoured by President Barack Obama as the National Young Entrepreneur of the Year for the sustained success of Gravity Payments. He was only 26 years old.

In response to the 2013 two–percent payroll tax reduction lapse in the US, Dan gave his employees a two–percent raise. Upon reading a 2010 study by Princeton University that concluded those who earn $75,000 or more are happier than those who earn less, Price reduced his $1 million salary to $70,000. This enabled him to raise his employees' annual salary to at least $70,000 for the next three years, even if it meant decreasing the company's annual profit of $2.2 million.

According to Price, "With leadership, there is a moral imperative for you to lead and do the right thing for those that you are leading." That moral imperative must either be sacrificial or it is simply a personal imperative.

3. THE LAW OF STRATEGY

"There is nothing as useless as doing efficiently that which should not be done at all." (Peter Drucker)

No example perfectly exemplifies what strategy is than the Battle of Normandy. Popularly known as D–Day, it was the most historic fight in the Second World War. Led by the U.S. Army General, Dwight Eisenhower, the allied forces were from the United States, United Kingdom, and Canada, as well as from Australia, Belgium, Czech Republic, France, Greece, the Netherlands, New Zealand, Norway and Poland. The operation was codenamed OVERLORD and was launched on June 6, 1944.

The success of D-Day required what we consider one of the most exceptional strategies to have ever been formulated by man. The purpose of D–Day may have been to infiltrate Europe with the allied forces, but the ultimate vision was to end World War II. This meant that the allied forces had to break through the forts of the very aggressive German army.

These objectives were all dependent on the success of the Battle of Normandy. Therefore, you can imagine the depth of planning that went into the strategy needed to ensure the execution was flawless. This is the Law of Strategy in action: to throw everything into the vision with no alternatives.

The word strategy originates from Greek and described commandership. This involved activities such as logistics, personnel, tactics, defence, deployment, etc., and in the case of the Battle of Normandy, the weather. The battle was initially planned for June 5th, 1944, but storms postponed the invasion to June 6th.

Strategy is plans that must be systematically executed to ensure the success of a grander vision. Strategy is so important that without it, leadership is like trying to shoot a terrified horsefly in a small pitch–dark room which is filled with mines.

If you are going to be successful in whatever in your life, you must adhere to the Law of Strategy. A plan may afford you a single meal, but if you wish to have three square meals a day, you must have a strategy. Do you even have an idea of how complicated it is to implement a vision that attracts people from all races and religions, from different ethics and ethnicity? This is what makes the Law of Strategy imperative.

The strategy which was used in the historic Battle of Normandy involved the coordination of almost three million troops from twelve nations, from the English Channel to the German–occupied territory of Normandy in France. This made it the largest invasion by sea in history. Sun Tzu once said, "All men can see these tactics whereby I conquer, but what none can see is the strategy out of which victory is evolved."

The most intelligent of all plans are sometimes obvious to the ignorant, but a well–thought out strategy will always elude the intelligence of the wise. To be effective in leadership requires a well–thought out strategy that combines a series of intelligent plans.

Most leadership challenges, which I have coached thousands of people on, would be inexistent if they simply had a strategy in place. Most had plans, desires, goals and objectives. They even had dedicated teams and enormous resources. However, they consistently breached the Law of Strategy. They didn't connect everything they were doing in support of the ultimate vision.

What most people don't realize is that the creation of the world is strategic, and that God has a strategy in place for everything in this world, which makes the cosmological theory for the birth of the universe, called the Big Bang, absolutely preposterous. It is the lack of strategy in this theory that makes it nonsense. Even the limited knowledge which human beings have of the universe indicate the intricacies that are perfectly working together to keep the universe going.

Science, which actually proves biblical claims than not, indicate that the distance of the sun from earth, is so perfectly calculated that if it were closer, earth would burn and if it were further, earth would freeze. This trumps the notorious idea of space being contained in a single point billions of years ago until it exploded.

As an entrepreneur, have you assessed the impact of absenteeism rate on your bottom line? As a CEO, what is your organizational strategy to ensure a steady climb in the satisfaction rate of your customers? As a pastor, what is your overall strategy to "feed the sheep" as instructed by your CEO, Jesus Christ?

As a parliamentarian, what part of your strategy is aimed at eliciting the support of your opponents who may be bent on frustrating the promises which your election victory is based on? This is an area President Barrack Obama is highly commended for his ability to gain the support of his rivals and even that of other nations for US–led initiatives.

President Obama's political strategy in 2008 included plans to use the social media to gain a forward momentum and generate excitement and donations for his campaign. Check. His strategy also included plans to engage the younger generation, who were not usually interested in politics, to gain their support. Check.

These, and other plans, which made up his overall strategy, enabled him to successfully secure the nomination of the Democratic Party against Hillary Clinton, who was the wife of one of America's most beloved presidents, and to finally beat John McCain, who was a seasoned politician, renowned activist and globally respected elder statesman.

Considering the remarkable odds that were stacked up against him, being an African–American who was a first–term Democratic senator from Illinois, and previously unheard of in other parts of the USA, President Obama broke every fundraising record for a presidential hopeful in his 2008 campaign to make history by raising $150 million and was elected the 44th President of the United States of America. This was the Law of Strategy in action.

FIVE COMPONENTS OF STRATEGY

"Without strategy, execution is aimless. Without execution, strategy is useless." (Morris Chang)

Since the Law of Strategy is the law that is most often breached, particularly by governments and churches, we will share more information to help you better understand it. Most leaders we have coached, trained or consulted in both of these institutions are challenged with the implementation of an effective strategy to support their vision. In a corporation, when the CEO outlines her strategy, the heads of departments have no alternative but to execute objectives that are related to the vision.

To ensure you have a robust strategy, here are the five critical elements that must be thoroughly examined, strategically planned and flawlessly executed in line with your strategic plan.

a. IDENTIFY A SPECIFIC TARGET

Be absolutely clear about the vision, what you wish to achieve and the mission, goals and objectives. If you are the visionary, ensure the vision is in line with the very purpose of your existence. If you are a supporter of someone else's vision, ensure that you completely understand what the person's vision is and identify how your talents may be used to support the vision.

All plans and activities must be aligned with this target. As Zig Ziglar said, "I don't care how much power, brilliance or energy you have, if you don't harness it and focus it on a specific target and hold it there, you are never going to accomplish as much as your ability warrants."

b. **DEVELOP APPLICABLE TACTICS**

Develop multidimensional plans for the different elements of your vision. This is where goals and objectives come in, as well as policies, processes and procedures. This is where you must determine the skill that you require. Despite the urgency of the mission, the planning for D–Day lasted more than a year. It took great effort for sea, air and ground troops from many nations to rehearse regularly. As General Eisenhower said, "I have always found that plans are useless, but planning is indispensable." In other words, strategy is the outcome of endless planning.

c. **FORM A COMPETENT TEAM**

Find competent people who complement each other with regards to their talents and skills. Simply hiring a qualified person to fill a vacant position is not strategic. But taking the time to find someone who may not be as qualified, but definitely possess a remarkable willingness to learn and most likely to stay longer with your organization is more strategic. If you don't get this right, nothing else will be right, for these are your ground troops and paratroopers. The ability to believe in yourself and others are the most critical aspect of leadership.

d. **ENSURE REGULAR TRAINING**

It is unfortunate to see how many organizations do not spend enough time and money to train the people who are meant to execute their vision. How long do you think your company will last without the continual training of your employees? Hiring the right people is only strategic if you plan to consistently enhance their skills and develop their talents. Churches should learn to train their congregations so they may excel in life and help to build the Kingdom.

Training is the process of educating people on what they must know to perform a task. As Richard Branson put it, "Train your people well enough so they can leave; treat them well enough so they don't want to." Regular training eventually translates to regular success, no matter what.

e. PUT PLANS TO TEST

Every experience is merely a test to reveal hidden opportunities for improvement. For your strategy to be effective, you must be willing to put it to the test. You must face the challenges and get the ball rolling, with an eye on the improvement opportunities. Strategy is like a game of chess, while the pawns are like plans; you must move them around to support your overall strategy, which, in chess, are the combined effort of the other pieces.

Sun Tzu was a general in the Chinese army as well as a strategist and philosopher. I strongly recommend his book *The Art of War* to everyone, particularly those in positions of authority. Here is Tzu's summary of the Law of Strategy:

In war, the general receives his commands from the sovereign. Having collected an army and concentrated his forces, he must blend and harmonize the different elements thereof before pitching his camp. After that, comes tactical manoeuvring, that which there is nothing more difficult. The difficulty of tactical maneuvering consists in turning the devious into the direct, and misfortune into gain. Thus, to take a long and circuitous route, after enticing the enemy out of the way, and though starting after him, to contrive to reach the goal before him, shows knowledge of the artifice of deviation. Maneuvering with an army is advantageous; but with an undisciplined multitude, most dangerous."

Spirituality is imperative. Sacrifice is required. Strategy is critical. Service is absolute.

4. THE LAW OF SERVICE

"The best way to find yourself is to lose yourself in the service of others." (Mahatma Gandhi)

Leadership is spirituality, sacrifice is the ultimate price for leadership and strategy is what enables success; however, service is the essence of leadership. For vision to be true, it must be about providing specific services that are beneficial to others. This is what makes the Law of Service a necessity in leadership; for where there is no service, there is no leadership.

What is the purpose of life if not to be of service to others? As Leo Rosten once said, "The purpose of life is not to be happy–but to matter, to be productive, to be useful, and to have it make some difference that you have lived at all." This is the Law of Service.

The Law of Service demands that service is at the forefront of your government, organization, church, community or college. It demands that you foster spirituality and make the sacrifices which are necessary to ensure the beneficiaries of your vision are, indeed, rendered the services that you deliver. Service may be complimentary or paid. It may come in the form of producing iPhones as Steve Job's Apple Inc. does or access to the basic needs that citizens expect of their government.

The depth of your spirituality, the level of your sacrifice and the effectiveness of your strategy are all measured by your adherence to the Law of Service.

The quality of service you provide will determine the duration of your vision, which in turn will determine the length of your leadership. Cutting corners to save cost or to avoid constructive feedback is detrimental to your leadership. Since service usually determines profitability in the corporate world, political leaders most often breach the Law of Service, for many of them make campaign promises with no intention of keeping them. To promise and not deliver negates your leadership. You are not a leader if you deliver below your capabilities. You are not leading until you serve others.

Like the other laws of leadership, the Law of Service is directly related to the Law of Spirituality. If your spirituality is immature, you will consistently breach this law. Every exceptional leader, whether political, religious, corporate or academic, is known for a specific service, for something that he consistently does so well. What are you known for? What is the quality of service that your organization provides to others? What is the strategy to consistently enhance your quality?

Leadership comes with pronounced and perceived expectations. The pronounced expectations are what you know about, while the perceived ones are what you should know about. The latter measures your performance, and the Law of Service requires you to fulfill both. In the words of Eugene B. Habecker, "The true leader serves. Serves people. Serves their best interests, and in doing so will not always be popular, may not always impress. But because true leaders are motivated by loving concern than a desire for personal glory, they are willing to pay the price."

Those on the Forbes' list of billionaires are noted for the exceptional services they deliver to the world and for the difference they make in the communities they operate.

There is a systematic approach to service which many people are unaware of, thus resulting in what Albert Einstein regarded as insanity: "Doing the same thing over and over again and yet expecting different results." One reason why some services are ineffective and unsustainable is because the lack of an effective strategy that is incongruent with the vision. Services are calculated activities that support your purpose, achieve your goals and objectives, and ultimately, advance your vision.

In some developing nations around the world, political leaders are known to seek medical care from western countries because the hospitals in their own countries are so dilapidated that admitted patients quickly die. Their political leaders use private jets for their long distance travel because corruption and neglect have bankrupted their national airlines.

They use police escorts on official and even personal engagements because of insecurity, rugged roads, pollution and chaotic traffic, while deplorable conditions have turned their highways to cemeteries. They send their children to schools overseas because the educational system in their own nations is in a perpetual state of disarray.

What is even more unfortunate is when some corporate and even religious leaders do the same. Some corporate officers offer the minimum of service, with no regard for quality or international standard, while accepting bribery and corruption as ways of doing business.

Even some religious servants, the very people we expect to strictly adhere to the Laws of Leadership, concern themselves with their own affairs rather than the needs of their people that they have gradually moved from being ineffective leaders to dictators. Nothing is more absurd than the claim to offer services that no one else finds valuable, not even you.

How exceptional are the services that you claim to provide? How loyal are you to the services you provide? How satisfied are those whom you claim to provide the services for? In case you are unaware, customer services has displaced price to become the number one reason why clients move their businesses to a company's competitors.

Therefore, the Law of Service is not only critical to your leadership but also to the profitability of your business. The chief executive officer of BlackBerry was recently embarrassed at a social function when people noticed that his wife was making calls with a Samsung phone instead of the expected Blackberry.

The Law of Service insists you provide the type of products and services that you will also be comfortable using. A leader does not offer anything less than what he would expect for himself. If it is not up to your own standard, why would you offer it to those who are paying you for it?

Exceptional Leaders are known to even have their meals in the same lunchroom with their employees, seizing every opportunity to test the quality of their products and services. Some have been known to periodically use the public washrooms just to ensure they are as clean as possible. Do you?

For service to impact and be sustainable, it must be strategically delivered with energy and as top priority. Service is a part of your leadership that can be measured objectively and it must be taken seriously. It is a part of your leadership that will demand your management capabilities to ensure the constant reengineering of your products and services.

The competition is so strong these days that it is no longer just what you deliver and why, but rather how you deliver the product. According to Mahatma Ghandi, "Service, which is rendered without joy, helps neither the servant nor the served. But all other pleasures and possessions pale into nothingness before service which is rendered in a spirit of joy."

Simply put, service can only be rendered from the heart when delivering what you were paid to do with your head.

5. THE LAW OF SUBSTANCE

"Morality is the basis of things and truth is the substance of all morality." (Mahatma Gandhi)

The Law of Substance requires you to strictly adhere to the other Laws of Leadership and foster the very essence of leadership, namely: a noble cause, positive energy, forward thinking and the advancement of humanity. As a leader, you should be open to change but also be very wary too, for not all change aligns with the essence of leadership. Substance is the actual matter of a thing, versus the fake, a look-alike or a shadow. It arises out of deep thought and reflection.

It is not what or who you know that will make you an exceptional leader, but rather what you are made of and what you stand for. In the words of Franz Kafka, "My 'fear' is my substance, and probably the best part of me." This should be your fear too, what you must protect at all cost. Your character sustains lasting impact upon others. The Law of Substance is not just an acute imperative in leadership, but the objective of everyone committed to the vision. Without it, you will stand for nothing and fall for everything.

When leaders lose their substance, they gradually become dictators. Dictators usually claim to stand for something, but in the end they only inflict pain and create anarchy. To lack substance is to be void of competence, compassion, commitment, consideration and cooperation. Substance is what makes leadership effective or ineffective. An absolute lack of substance creates dictatorship. As Edmund Burke put it, "All human laws are, properly speaking, only declaratory; they have no power over the substance of original justice."

The Law of Substance requires that all you say and do is reflective of the undergirding moral foundations. When you complain, make excuses and blame other people, you break this law. When you are swayed by polls rather than by principles, by change rather than by character, you breach this law.

The Law of Substance will protect your leadership, for it will compel you to develop your character, be considerate towards others and remain focused on your vision. Nelson Mandela was able to weather his storm for twenty-seven years because he was a man of substance. Had he not been, he would have quickly given into the pressure to renounce his vision.

Sadly, I learned in my research, political leaders typically breach the Law of Substance more often than corporate leaders, which is why Nelson Mandela's sacrifice is outstanding. Politicians are more prone to negotiate for positions that suit themselves and their political agenda than corporate leaders are. It is more likely for a politician to make a promise during campaign and break it after being elected than it is for a CEO of a Fortune 500 company to layout objectives only to disregard them after an annual general meeting.

Before assuming a position of authority, ensure that you have built and tested your character. Make certain you are able to rise above the natural inclinations for popularity, prosperity and power, and that you are unwilling to negotiate your principles.

In the words of Henry A. Kissinger, "High office teaches decision making, not substance. It consumes intellectual capital; it does not create it. Most high officials leave office with the perceptions and insights with which they entered; they learn how to make decisions but not what decisions to make."

When challenges and difficulties arise, the Law of Substance will sustain you. If you are without it, the slightest wind will blow you away.

Your adherence to the Law of Substance will enable you to develop your character through patience and perseverance. It will enable you to command the respect you need in order to sustain the excitement of those who are attracted to your vision. A person of substance makes decisions based on conviction and character, not on polls and perceptions.

This law requires you to stand for something significant, meaningful, progressive, compassionate and revolutionary. Without substance, there is no character; and without character, there is no leadership.

The idea of same–sex marriage, for instance, lacks sense and substance because it obviously breaches the natural law upon which God instituted marriage. The fact that two people of the same sex believe they are in love with each other may necessitate a change to the man–made constitution but does not change the sacred understanding of marriage.

Freedom is everyone's right, but so is foolishness. Moral decadence has led many people to do whatever they want so long as their actions do not infringe on the rights of others. However, if you are uncertain of your beliefs, or reject natural laws because of societal pressure, you lack substance and character, you defy this law.

Abraham Lincoln, Martin Luther King Jr. and Mother Teresa are iconic leaders precisely because of their admirable adherence to the Law of Substance. Although some suggest a leader's role is to implement change; however, that is not always the case, especially when change contradicts natural laws and undermines a leader's character and beliefs.

Anyone can implement change and should be open to change, but it takes a person of character to stand up against change that contradicts the essence of leadership. Your charisma may bring people together, but it is your character that will keep them together.

Your character determines your substance, and nothing develops your character more than trials and tribulations of life. An accurate reflection of your character is how you behave in the face of oppression, opposition and obstruction. When you respond to hate with hate, aggression with aggression, and selfishness with selfishness, you violate the Law of Substance.

You disregard the Law of Substance if you live life in such a way that only you seem to matter, without showing love and kindness to your neighbours and without thinking of your purpose in life and the need for continual personal development.

In the words of Dr. Myles Munroe, "No one should think he is too smart or too safe to avoid the consequences of a lack of character." Success in life is based on nothing other than a focused mind, gentle spirit and an unwavering character.

To avoid violating the Law of Substance, you must establish a set of values, morals, ethics and principles and make firm commitment to adhere to them, no matter what the cost may be. Could you even imagine how many times Nelson Mandela must have been tempted to sign his release papers if he would renounce his vision?

Recently declassified information in the U.S. revealed many threats and blackmails against Martin Luther King Jr.. Despite those threats, Martin Luther King Jr. remained a man of substance until death. Women and men revere him, even fifty years after his death, because of his character and not for his position, popularity, prosperity, population or power.

6. THE LAW OF SUCCESS

"Always bear in mind that your own resolution to succeed is more important than any other." (Abraham Lincoln)

In two decades, I have given nearly a thousand keynote addresses on the topic of success and have heard a thousand more from other speakers. I have trained, coached and mentored people on it and responded to thousands of questions about it through our websites and social media sites. It is one of the most frequently discussed subjects and yet few know what success really is.

However, one thing is certain: you can never be successful in life until you take it in your own hands. You are the driver of your success. Your success depends on whether you fulfill your purpose or not and whether you advanced your vision in the best possible way.

The Law of Success is a critical part of leadership; otherwise, what is the purpose of leading if not to accomplish a goal and vision. Many violate the Law of Success due to their misunderstanding of what success means, and not necessarily because of incompetence or defiance.

If you think leadership is about position, popularity, prosperity, population and power, then you will end up measuring your success according to these vices of leadership. You would naively consider yourself successful when you eventually achieve them; but unfortunately, they are not valid measures of success.

Success is simply the accomplishment of the goals that are associated with a specific vision. Personal goals, which you are encouraged to set for yourself, may include becoming the governor of your state or a mayor. However, the measure of your leadership effectiveness must be strictly align with the original purpose of leadership, which is to execute a vision that is greater than you and positively impact humanity.

As Les Brown, the globally–renowned motivational speaker often says, "The problem is not that people don't set goals, but rather, they set goals that are too low and achieve."

Leadership goals are different from management goals. If, as the CFO of your organization, your goal is to reduce cost by twenty–five percent, that is a management goal, and not the measure of success of your leadership. If becoming CEO in three years is your goal, then it is a professional goal. If life balance is your goal, then is a personal goal.

But the goals and objectives of leadership are different from these. Whether you are a clerk, clergy or captain, the ultimate goal of a leader is to advance a vision from one specific point to another. This can only be done by fulfilling your purpose in life, and inform, influence and inspire others to discover and fulfill their purpose in life as well. Every other goal you have should enable you to achieve this one.

The measurement of success in leadership is strictly about the vision and the people it attracts and not about polls, perceptions and profits. The vision must be advancing and the people must be maximizing their talents or else your leadership is ineffective, which will be a breach in the Law of Success.

As Henry Ford said, "The whole secret of a successful life is to find out what is one's destiny to do, and then do it." Success in leadership is a blunt refusal to not compromise in your integrity and your principles, even if it may result in the loss of your position, popularity, prosperity, population and power.

THE SEVEN PRINCIPLES OF SUCCESS

"Success is not final; failure is not fatal. It is the courage to continue that counts." (Winston Churchill)

Success is simply the conquest of many challenges. This means there can be no success without challenge. In fact, challenges breed success. If you desire success in life, leadership and love, you must be willing to face the challenges that hinder your progress in these areas. You should have an unabashed quest for the knowledge you need, a contagious passion for the hard work ahead of you and an unconditional love for everyone, including those who care less about you.

In the words of Oprah Winfrey, "My philosophy is that not only are you responsible for your life, but doing the best at this moment puts you in the best place for the next moment."

As in leadership and other critical aspects of life, the idea of success is ridden with misconceptions. Due to its complex nature, it is beneficial to outline some hard facts about success. Like the Seven Organic Laws of Leadership, these Principles of Success are not subject to change. They are consistent and applicable in every area of life, including business and relationships.

i. The Key to Success is in Your Hand

Regardless of your situation or the challenges you face, you are only going to be as rich as you're prudent, as smart as your willing to learn and as happy as you are quick to forgive. People will try to hinder you, but with patience and perseverance, success is inevitable. The challenges that you experience today are meant to prepare you to conquer the ones ahead of you tomorrow.

ii. Success is Your Birthright

You were created for a purpose and blessed with the talents to fulfil it. Success, therefore, was entrusted to you before birth and demanded of you before death. You simply need to be who you are called to be. Success is inevitable if you work hard on your goals and objectives that are in line with your purpose in life. In fact, it is in God's best interest for you to succeed. Whatever you were created for, you are bound to succeed in if you dedicate yourself to it.

iii. Success is Measured by Self

It is a misconception to measure personal success by comparing yourself to anyone, for nothing determines your success but the accomplishment of the goals and objectives that are in line with your purpose. In other words, you may have no position, popularity, prosperity, population and power and yet be successful simply because you achieved the very purpose for which you were created. Simply put, success is the fulfillment of your purpose in life.

iv. Success is Contentment

Success is contentment with or without riches. It is what you set out to achieve that determines your success. You set the goal, you do the work and you decide both the input and output. But you must fulfill your purpose in life to be successful. Good enough is not good enough; neither is great nor even greatest. You achieve greatness simply by aligning everything you do with your purpose in life. This is the success that leads to fulfillment.

v. Success is Overrated

Success is unfortunately a buzzword commonly used to signify the rich and famous, when, in essence, it is simply the fulfillment of your purpose in life. That may or may not include being famous and rich. The world promotes this misconception and many buy into it, but as long as you are focused on the pursuit of your purpose, and advancement of your vision, you are successful. No financial or academic achievement can compensate for a life devoid of purpose.

vi. Success is About Knowledge

Success is more about what you know than whom you know; more about how you think than what you do. You do not get from life what you put into it; but rather, you get from life what you know and how much you think things through. It is the knowledge of life that will enable you to navigate through the valley of challenges to reach the peak of your existence. Many people put everything into life and yet achieve nothing out of it because they focused on everything else but their purpose in life. What you know about your life purpose guarantees success.

vii. Success is Dependent

Contrary to popular notion, you cannot achieve success alone, but rather through collaboration and cooperation. The Bible consistently refers to "one another," a strong indication that human beings are meant to work together to achieve their individual success. Businesses need customers and customers need business. Michael Jordan and Wayne Gretzky owe their successes to their coaches and teammates. A leader cannot become exceptional by working alone, but rather by his ability to influence and inspire everyone to work together.

To ignore the Law of Success is both a waste of time and an absolute disregard for your vision. It is this law that guarantees the continuation of your vision. This is the law that will compel you to continually forge ahead, to be mindful of your performance and that of those who are attracted to your vision, versus their true potential. The Law of Success requires you to have faith instead of fear, to focus instead of worry.

In the words of Brian Tracy, "Winners make a habit of manufacturing their own positive expectations in advance of the event."

If you desire fulfillment in life, you must adhere to the Law of Success, for it is the eventual outcome of a series of successful activities that work together for the advancement of your vision. You will encounter some setbacks along the way, but they are merely opportunities to prepare you for amazing comebacks.

Failure is only an indication that success is definitely ahead of you; therefore, you must not waver in your purpose or tire in your quest when you fall short.

Nothing is impossible until you say so, for impossibility is a strong indication of possibility. As for me, success is my only option. I have heard of failure many times, but I am not interested in it.

7. THE LAW OF SUCCESSION

"The final test of a leader is that he leaves behind him in other men the conviction and will to carry on." (Walter J. Lippmann)

The Seventh Organic Law of Leadership is the Law of Succession, the law that ensures the continuity of your vision when you are long gone. The Law of Succession is the reason Apple can boast of its continuous success after the passing of the visionary Steve Jobs. Without question, Steve Jobs prepared Tim Cook to be his successor well before he died. You violate the sixth law, the Law of Success, if you do not prepare a successor to continue the vision. For, what is success, if the vision dies with you?

Since we do not always have the privilege of knowing the time or season of death as Jobs did, then we must identify our successor from the beginning. The essence of leadership is not power, but to empower others. Thus, when a leader passes on without preparing a successor to advance the vision, the leader has defied the Law of

Succession. The greatest tragedy of this is the loss of a leader's vision and legacy.

One of the greatest leadership dilemmas in corporations and churches today is the lack of a succession plan. What makes this even more critical is that most leaders do not even consider the Law of Succession, while others who do, have no contingency or business continuity plans in place.

In the words of Dr. Myles Munroe, "The greatest obligation of a true leader is to transfer a deposit into the next generation. The worst mistake a leader can make is to mentor no one, choose no successor and leave no legacy."

Once you assume leadership of anything, your first priority should be to build a team of competent people who understands the vision, aware of their individual purpose in life, know how to maximize their talents in support of the vision and are willing to constantly develop their related skills.

Your second priority should be to identify your successor and bring him along as much as possible to increase his awareness, excitement, understanding and determination. You may have to go through a few candidates before being certain of the right one, which is why you begin today.

The benefits of a succession plan cannot be overemphasized. In fact, everything you have accomplished in life can only be meaningful if they are in line with your purpose in life and in support of a vision that will outlive you. This is the definition of legacy.

The Law of Succession guarantees the advancement of your vision when you are long gone. It protects your legacy and ensures your effort blesses the next generation. This is one of the reasons why God commissioned us to go into the world and multiply: not just offspring, but also mentees and successors to continue our vision and legacy.

Research indicates that it is costly to hire new employees. That amount doubles exponentially if the new employees are meant to assume critical positions of authority in their organizations with no effective transfer of knowledge. Based on the positions or authority, it may take incumbents up to five years to acquire the priceless knowledge of their predecessors. This is why it is essential for you to adhere to this law.

It is a tragedy how many legacies are torn apart because great visionaries breached the Law of Succession. It is equally unfortunate to see major corporations disintegrate because a visionary died without preparing a successor. In the same way, churches have broken up because junior pastors sought the most senior position immediately after the senior pastor's departure. Yet Jesus Christ, the CEO of churches, consistently mentored Peter throughout His ministry. Jesus identified, selected, confirmed, trained and mentored Peter. Upon His resurrection, Jesus affirmed Peter and informed, influenced and inspired him to continue on His vision.

Succession planning is a rigorous process designed to effectively manage and mitigate the impact of a leader's departure on the vision. The plan is for the visionary to instil his vision into the heart and mind of his successor and then implement development initiatives to enable the successor's readiness to advance the vision. While it is critical for leaders to dedicate enough time to mentor their successors, few leaders actually do; this is alarming, if not disappointing.

Unlike a sole proprietor who can determine his successor, the CEO of a corporation may groom a junior executive to assume the leadership of the corporation, but that is subject to the company's board of directors. In the same way, the mayor of a city or even the president of a nation may implement a succession plan in the favour of a preferred candidate, but it is still subject to the electorate.

If the spirit of leadership has been ignited in you, do you have a succession plan? Who are you mentoring right now to advance your vision? What level of influence do you have over your successor? If it is high, do you have a plan to minimize the impact of your departure? Don't you know that the truest test of your leadership is what happens to your accomplishments after you leave?

As Dr. Myles Munroe puts it, "No matter how much you may learn, achieve, accumulate, or accomplish, if it all dies with you, then you are a generational failure."

The Law of Succession is not an item on a checklist; rather, it is what must be built into the culture of an organization, government or church. It is an absolute requirement for exceptional leadership and for those who strongly desire to sustain their legacy. The ultimate measurement of your leadership success is based on this the Law of Succession.

Implementation of this law in your organization will determine the longevity of your vision. An excellent team member must be groomed for the role of a CEO to ensure the continuation of the vision. The same is true for churches, regardless of how small the congregations.

My research shows that most leaders fail to implement succession plans because they do not trust other's motives and abilities to advance the vision. This translates into a fear of losing what they spent their lives building. Some leaders have people in mind, but those people are either not interested or unwilling to prepare themselves.

Other leaders claim to have not identified potential successors at all, which calls their leadership into question. If you have been driving a vision for a minimum of three years and do not have a potential successor in mind or in place, the vision is already at risk and your legacy in jeopardy. You are already in breach of this law and must begin this process without delay.

A succession plan is not a nice thing to have, but rather a must have. It is not optional, but rather the condition upon which the continuity of your vision is dependent. Everyone in your organization must be made to see the value of having a backup person and not just a backup plan; a backup plan is useless if it does not identify a backup person to execute it in the case of a leader's departure. This is not just for those in high levels of authority, but also for customer service representatives, sales officers, and even mailroom staff.

It is even required at home!

FRAMEWORK FOR SUCCESSION PLANNING

"The best way to predict the future is to create it." (Abraham Lincoln)

For a succession plan to be effective, it must be strategically developed, effectively communicated and tactfully executed. Considering the aging workforce of today, increasing turnover rates, complexities of work and lagging loyalty between employees and the organizations they work for, it would be unwise to not have succession plans in place. According to an ancient Chinese proverb, "A person who does not worry about the future will shortly have worries about the present." The future, therefore, is the outcome of preparations made in the present.

Based on the criticality of the Law of Succession, I developed a framework in the form of a seven–step process. This framework streamlines the succession planning process to enable its maximum effectiveness within an eighteen-month period; although, I strongly recommend that the seventh phase continues for up to three years. Regardless of the position and type of organization, whether a corporation, sole proprietorship or church, this framework is sufficient to protect the future of your vision when you move or pass on.

i. IDENTIFICATION

This is the phase whereby the key positions that must be included in the succession plan are identified. The dependencies of these key roles must also be clearly mapped out. This will help to articulate the impact that the positions have on the vision and on each other. If the CFO is being groomed for the position of CEO, someone else should be groomed simultaneously for the position of CFO, since both positions of authority usually work closely together.

It is beneficial for potential candidates to already have working relationships with each other. This will help avoid common instances whereby the implementation of succession plans creates dissension among peers. Organizations that fail to factor this interdependency into their succession plan unfortunately create detrimental gaps and lapses in their corporate communications and expectations. In some cases, this oversight split the organization into warring groups before eventually bringing it down altogether.

ii. SELECTION

In this phase, candidates are carefully selected for the key positions identified in Phase 1. It is an even more delicate process than Phase 1; therefore, it must be done diligently and discreetly without letting the candidates or the organization know. In addition to being academically and experientially qualified, the recommended criteria for the selection process are as follows:

- They must fully understand the vision and are remarkably passionate about it.
- They must have discovered their purpose in life and definitely know how it fits into the vision of the organization.
- They must have ignited their leadership spirit and have consistently demonstrated outstanding leadership abilities and management skills.
- They must embrace and be energized about The Seven Organic Laws of Leadership.
- They must have your trust and the trust of your peers and strategic colleagues.

iii. CONFIRMATION

This is the phase whereby the selected candidates undergo a series of covert training programs to test their capabilities and readiness. This process may include getting them involved in projects and initiatives that may be outside their realm of responsibility in order to test their ability, aptitude and attitude.

They may also be tactfully asked to fill in for others who are away or to job shadow in roles related to those which they are being groomed for. This will enable you to get other people's perspectives without divulging the intention.

iv. INFORMATION

At this stage, candidates who were successful in Phase 2 are formally notified through an interview process that they are being considered for the position. This will ensure that they are interested in the role and ready for the next steps.

They should be strongly advised to carefully examine themselves with regards to the natural tendencies for position, popularity, prosperity, population and power. They should also be made aware of the potential impact of the role on their lives and families.

v. EDUCATION

This is the phase whereby enthusiastic candidates undergo formal training that could not have been done covertly in Phase 3. They should be exposed to the policies, processes, procedures and perspectives that may not be part of their regular responsibilities, but are required for the identified roles.

This education must include informal initiatives such as introducing them to key contacts and inviting them to the type of meetings, events and functions that are associated with the role.

However, both the organization and candidate still have the right to opt out of the succession-planning program should this phase unveil any incompatibility which is considered significant enough to hinder the candidate's later success.

vi. EXAMINATION

This is the phase whereby successful candidates undergo rigorous examination, whether formal or informal. If any certification program is required, it must be completed in this phase.

Time must be created for these candidates to test their readiness for the position. The examination process should include the key associates of the position and end with formal acknowledgement of success.

vii. ACTUALIZATION

Finally, at this stage, the successful candidate from Phase 6 is formally recognized as the successor for the respective position. This is the most formal process in this framework, as it must include formal documentation and agreement of mutual expectations, accountabilities and responsibilities.

In this final phase, the right to opt out of the succession program is limited. There must be clearly articulated consequences. When the agreement is in place, the incumbents must be recognized as such and given regular opportunities to demonstrate their competence in the new role. They must be copied on selected communications and their opinions solicited in strategic and tactical matters that are considered valuable knowledge for the role.

Succession planning is not a simple process, but rather a complex one. It must be initiated as soon as you ignite your leadership spirit, create your vision or assume a position of authority. Some entrepreneurs have been in business for decades and are unable to boast of a loyal team.

I remember taking a walk with Dr. Myles Munroe through his organization during my visit with him in the Bahamas. As his staff said hello with a smile one after the other, he would ask them how long they have been working with him. Every answer was in decades; some for 15 years, others, 20, 25 and even for 30 years!

Just as I was trying to comprehend the magnitude of this mentorship walk, he said, "You see, most of my team members have been with me for decades. This is what it takes to succeed in business and ministry. You must build a team of loyal and passionate people who are willing to continue advancing the vision when you pass on."

If you are not able to build a team of loyal people, you will not be able to implement a succession plan. Some Fortune 500 companies are beginning to understand the significance of "a team of loyal people" that executives are now attentive to the attrition rate of their organizations. No other performance indicator measures your leadership effectiveness more than this.

While the reason for attrition varies, an increasing rate is a cause for alarm. A high attrition rate indicates the amount of knowledge that is migrating out of your organization. Attrition is one of the foremost hindrances to succession plans. Regardless of the effectiveness of your succession plan, it is at the mercy of your attrition rate. Organizations that ignore this measurement are blinded to the reality of their organization, for you are either growing steadily or dying gradually. The attrition rate of your company will make it clear to you.

Depending on the size of your organization, a succession planning committee may have to be set up to ensure due diligence in each phase. This committee must be discreet in their approach, especially in Phases 2 and 3. This will mitigate misunderstanding among the employees, as some may see it as impending restructuring or retrenchment.

If you know your organization as much as you should, Phases 1 and 2 may be considered quick wins and can be completed in one and two months respectively. Phase 3 may be completed in three months, leaving a year to execute Phases 4 to 7. This will allow you eighteen months to implement the plan.

Since Phase 4 focuses on discussion and reflection, it can be done in two months, while Phases 5, 6 and 7 many be completed in five, three and two months respectively. Most of the work is in Phase 5, as it is dependent on the depth of knowledge transfer that must occur.

A sole proprietor would likely require less time to complete this phase than the CEO of a major corporation. Regardless, this is the phase where leaders should make themselves completely dispensable, something most leaders fail to do because of the natural tendencies for position, popularity, prosperity, population and power.

The Law of Succession is the law that will either make or break your legacy. If you have not yet identified a successor to advance your vision, you may take a break from reading this book and immediately use this framework to implement a succession plan. As John C. Maxwell once said, "Leadership is influence. Leaders who mentor potential leaders multiply their effectiveness. There is no success without a successor."

Without succession, therefore, leadership fails. If you so strongly believe in your vision, and consider the effort you have put into it thus far to be worthwhile, implement your succession plan now.

These Seven Organic Laws of Leadership summarizes the knowledge, habits and behaviours of the iconic leaders who I diligently studied. These Seven Organic Laws of Leadership are interconnected. Although, the first one, which is the Law of Spirituality, is the foundation for the rest, while the success of your leadership depends on the last one, namely, the Law of Succession. According to James C. Hunter, "The degree to which we choose to deviate from the laws of human nature is the degree to which we get off course and begin to run aground."

Chapter Four

The Leadership Manifesto

–Ten Characteristics of Exceptional Leaders

> "Character is like a tree and reputation is like its shadow. The shadow is what we think of it; the tree is the real thing."
> –Abraham Lincoln

A characteristic is a feature or quality that distinguishes one person or thing from another; usually it is an original mark, a natural talent, a peculiar trait or remarkable attribute that a person or thing possesses, but not the other that is being compared. Characteristics are often used to tell the differences between people or things, not their similarities. In fact, people and things are defined by their characteristics. They are clues—you can tell what is being described simply by its characteristics.

A lion and a sheep are both four–legged animals; however, they are not the same animal. While they are both mammals, they possess distinctive qualities that set them apart from each other. They are so different that they are sworn enemies of each other. Similarly, both the eagle and the chicken belong to the class of vertebrates comprising of birds and both belong to the same phylum, namely chordata. This means that they have a single dorsal nerve and many others similarities in their body plan. However, rather than similarities, it is their characteristics that set them apart.

For a trait to be considered a characteristic, it must set you apart from the others of your kind. It must make you unique enough to stand out among your peers. Instead of comparing the lion and the sheep, a fair comparison is the lion and the tiger. Both belong to the genus of the five big cats and are vicious predators. Despite their numerous similarities, it is their characteristics that make them unique. The lion is usually faster than the tiger by up to twenty miles per hour, and also usually found in Africa, while the tiger is usually found in Asia.

So it is in leadership as well; what sets exceptional leaders apart from the rest is the following set of ten characteristics. These ten characteristics of leadership are grounded in psychological, physiological, spiritual and philosophical research. I thoroughly reviewed and discovered these characteristics in the lives of exceptional leaders regardless of their calling. While some people may be unaware of these ten characteristics, they are the most obvious characteristics that turned ordinary people into the exceptional leaders we adore today.

When comparing two people, with the intention of identifying the characteristics that sets them apart from each other, you should focus on their differences and not their similarities. It is only proper to focus on their respective distinctive traits instead of their obvious commonalities. Instead of saying they are both human beings, you could say that one is a female while the other is a male since characteristics are what makes the male and female different. These ten characteristics will set you apart from your peers, whether you hold a position of authority or not.

Regardless of the magnitude of your vision, the longstanding dreams that keep you awake at night or the difference you wish to make in the world, these are the ten characteristics that will ignite and sustain your leadership spirit. In fact, if you wish to become exceptional in leadership, you must consider these characteristics as commandments. A command is a mandate that must be done, without exception, to achieve a definite result.

Your character is a culmination of your habits. To change your character, you must change your habits. To change your habits, you must follow a set of definite principles that were delicately put together to influence your mindset and behaviour. Upon leading the Israelites out of their bondage in Egypt, God gave Moses the Ten Commandments to help them unlearn the detrimental habits and learn beneficial habits to develop a spiritual and strategic mindset.

As you go through these characteristics one by one, pause along the way to ask yourself how well you are doing in each of them. This is where you get to actually measure your leadership performance or your readiness for leadership. If you have yet to ignite your leadership spirit or assume a position of authority in a church, corporation, college or government, these commandments will provoke your thoughts, challenge your outlook on everything and expose opportunities for your personal development.

This Leadership Manifesto is not a suggestion for exceptional leadership, but rather an imperative for those who wish to fulfill their purpose in life, those who wish to advance a vision that would impact humanity and leave a legacy for following generations.

These Ten Commandments of Leadership are evident in the lives of exceptional leaders. They are vital rules for your own leadership development, and must be embraced with a contagious excitement and unwavering dedication.

1. YOU SHALL HAVE A PURPOSE FOR YOUR VISION

"The purpose of life is not to be happy–but to matter, to be productive, to be useful, and to have it make some difference that you have lived at all." (Leo Rosten)

No one is more fulfilled in life than a person of purpose and no other character defines a leader more that the definitiveness of purpose. Purpose generates passion and passion inspires vision, which in turn, ignites the leadership spirit that is required to advance the vision. If any word is a synonym for leadership, it is purpose. Your leadership spirit can only be ignited the moment you make the ultimate decision to live for a purpose that would impact humanity.

Without a definite sense of purpose, your leadership spirit will not be ignited. Until you are absolutely sure of what your purpose in life is, and how that purpose fits into a vision that would impact the world for good, your leadership spirit will lay dormant. You may hold a position of authority, be regarded a genius by your peers, or have amassed wealth and knowledge beyond measure, but if uncertain about your purpose in life, your leadership spirit cannot be ignited.

Purpose is not just a mere thought or an idea; it is a fact of life and the truth about you. Your purpose is not what you or other people think you were created for, but rather what you were specifically created for by God. If you pursue any purpose other than the exact purpose that God created you for, your leadership spirit will lay dormant. You may assume a position of authority, but unable to demonstrate exceptional leadership.

Life is meaningful only with a sense of purpose. Purpose is what you were created to fulfill in life, while vision is how the fulfillment of your purpose would look like when it is all said and done. Purpose is what you must live for, while vision is what you must be willing to die for. If unwilling to subject yourself to your purpose in life, you will end up eating from the table of mediocrity.

If you pass away without fulfilling your purpose in life, you will not have lived at all, for it is the fulfillment of purpose that gives life meaning. No challenge, pain, hurt or disappointment has consequences greater than that of life without purpose. If your vision is not aligned with your purpose in life, your vision is merely a pie in the sky. Without purpose, leadership is inexistent. Your leadership spirit can only be ignited when you embrace your purpose in life.

I founded the School of Greatness strictly to enable millions of people to discover and fulfill their individual purpose in life. The first of its kind, this school uses a robust infrastructure to facilitate seminars and webinars on life, leadership and entrepreneurial skills that are expected of everyone but not taught in conventional schools.

My purpose in life is to inspire and enable people to discover and fulfill their purpose in life. It is this purpose that I have relentlessly pursued for decades; it gave birth to the vision of the School of Greatness. Since the virtual doors opened in 2013, I have been able to reach over 100,000 people in over 45 countries.

THE POWER OF PURPOSE

"The secret to success is constancy of purpose." (Benjamin Disraeli)

To ascertain the respective life purpose of iconic leaders who the world adores today, all we have to do is thoroughly examine what they eventually died for. Upon his historic release from captivity, Nelson Mandela won the election to become the first president of the country, in the first fully representative democratic election. He was also the first person of African heritage to head the country.

At the time of his death on December 5, 2013, at the age of 95, he had "fought the good fight, finished the race and kept the faith", just as the apostle Paul said before he also passed away. Mandela did not hold on to the position and power of the presidency, which he could have without question, but rather stepped down after just a term. He had fulfilled his purpose in life and remarkably advanced his vision to the highest level possible. That was his destiny.

Mandela did not waste his five years in office lamenting the injustice of his imprisonment and racial prejudice against his people. He spent it to dismantle the legacy of apartheid, focus on racial reconciliation and tackled inequality, poverty and the lack of education and health care, which the racist regimes had denied his people for generations.

He was always a man on a mission and when he had fulfilled his purpose, he diligently laid down the groundwork for the next generation to continue the transformation and then gladly passed on the baton. Dr. Myles Munroe did the same thing as well, for, even though he passed on suddenly, he made the necessary leadership transition. Today, his children, Charisa and Cairo (Myles Jr.) are travelling around the world teaching the leadership philosophies of their father.

Mandela's purpose was crystal–clear, his consistent passion and unwavering principle. Due to his nobility, he turned down many opportunities to flee from South Africa. Rather he chose to stand up for his beliefs even though it threatened to cost him his life and freedom. Mandela writes, "During my lifetime I have dedicated myself to this struggle of the African people. I have fought against white domination, and I have fought against black domination. I have cherished the ideal of a democratic and free society in which all persons live together in harmony and with equal opportunities. It is an ideal which I hope to live for and to achieve. But if need be, it is an ideal for which I am prepared to die."

So what is your purpose in life? How does your purpose fit into your profession? Is your career in line with your calling? To discover your purpose in life, you have to examine your life from its beginning to now, with a focus on what pains you the most. Based on our experiences from coaching and mentoring thousands of people through their life and business challenges, we discovered that in your story is your glory: your challenges are your opportunities, your mess is your miracle, and your pain, is your purpose.

An exceptional leader is consistently purposeful in his approach. He does not have the luxury of speaking without consciousness and acting without consideration. He must have unwavering integrity, utmost diligence and an unswerving focus. This is the lot in the life of an exceptional leader–his determination to fulfill his purpose in life and dedication to enable others to do the same, even if it means enormous sacrifices.

You are pregnant with something of great value to the world, whether it is a ground–breaking dream, a significant goal, a definite purpose. Until you give birth to this purpose, your leadership spirit will not be ignited. You may have held positions of authority for years, but until you embrace your purpose in life, your achievements will be unsustainable. When you choose a purpose–driven life, those who are meant to be around you will start becoming more productive.

In the pursuit of purpose, there will be some overwhelming challenges and even some casualties, but fulfillment is also guaranteed. A purpose–driven life is what creates exceptional leaders out of ordinary people. Until you are deeply troubled by pain or the lack of something that would make a great difference to humanity, you will neither be motivated to fulfill your purpose in life, nor give birth to a vision that would eventually create a legacy for you.

The iconic leaders we adore today are all remembered for the significant purpose for which they lived and not for their position, popularity, prosperity, population and power.

HOW TO DISCOVER YOUR PURPOSE

"Life is an endless process of self-discovery." (James Gardner)

The course on how to discover purpose in life is the most requested of the School of Greatness. In fact, it is a prerequisite for the other programs we offer in the institution. Without knowing your purpose in life, nothing else matters, not even what truly matter. In the words of George Bernard Shaw, "This is the true joy of life, the being used for a purpose recognized by yourself as a mighty one; the being thoroughly worn out before you are thrown on the scrap heap."

Lack and pain are the incubators of purpose. Until you are troubled by the lack of something that would be beneficial to mankind, you will not become pregnant with your purpose in life, you will not be able to give birth to a vision that would eventually create a legacy for you.

To discover your purpose in life, therefore, you must first determine what pains you the most in life. What is your most painful experience in life and what are your natural talents that can be leveraged to protect others from the same pain?

Moses' pain was the suffering of the Israelites in Egypt. In realizing that, his purpose was revealed. Martin Luther King Jr.'s pain was the injustice against the African American, thus his purpose was to fight for a free and fair America.

Profession and purpose possess unique characteristics that set them apart. Despite the prevailing misconception that profession and purpose are the same thing, their respective characteristics indicate otherwise. As I often say to youth when speaking at universities and colleges, the only way you find fulfillment in your profession is to ensure it is aligned with your purpose in life. If not, you will be gradually working your way to be among the eighty percent of people who are unfulfilled at work, despite their robust pay package.

Satisfaction is temporal, while fulfillment is permanent. Satisfaction can be derived from many things in life, but nothing, absolutely nothing will give you fulfillment in life more than a definitiveness of purpose.

A medical doctor may be satisfied with her six-figure salary and the prestige, privileges and perks of her profession, but she will be unfulfilled in life if her purpose is not related to the medical field. God endowed us with the natural talents we require to fulfill our purpose in life, while the abilities we need to excel in our profession (and purpose) must be learned.

If the medical doctor's purpose is to advance the vision of finding cure for cancer, then her becoming a medical doctor becomes very relevant in her journey. She would often approach her job with unceasing passion and unwavering principle because her professional excellence is necessary to fulfill her purpose and advance her vision for humanity.

Imagine having being influenced by your parents to become an accountant because your father is one, only to find out that your life purpose is to advance the search for the cure for cancer, especially since you lost three loved ones to it. You may become the CFO of Cancer Foundation, but if your purpose is to be in the field of research, if the pain of losing three loved ones is fuelling your passion, what was the essence of studying accounting in the first place?

The misconception that profession and purpose is the same thing is a significant reason why almost eighty percent of employees are unfulfilled at work. Many may be satisfied with their salary and work environment, but remain unfulfilled in life.

I have learned that while your profession has more control over you, you have more control over your purpose. Furthermore, while your profession may lead to retirement, your purpose leads to your legacy, since there is no retirement in purpose. In the words of King Solomon, "Many are the plans in a person's heart, but it is the Lord's purpose that prevails."

Everyone knows Bill Gates for his ground–breaking innovation in the field of technology, but few know that he was a law student at Harvard University with plans of becoming a lawyer like his father. Everyone remembers Steve Jobs for revolutionizing many industries in the technology world, but few know that he enrolled at Reeds College because he wanted something that was more artistic and interesting.

If Gates and Jobs had pursued professions through the college programs they initially enrolled for, they may have likely become excellent in law and arts respectively. However, imagine how far behind the world would have been without their intense pursuit of purpose.

Purpose is critical to living and non–living things. Without purpose, there is nothing. Nothing, absolutely nothing, exists without a purpose. But make no mistake about it, purpose can only be determined by the creator of the creation; in our case, as humans, by God. This means that to discover your purpose in life requires an encounter with God.

According to Rick Warren, the author of *The Purpose–Driven Life*, "Without God, life has no purpose, and without purpose, life has no meaning. Without meaning, life has no significance or hope." A divine purpose, therefore, is the hallmark of exceptional leadership.

2. YOU SHALL FOSTER PRINCIPLES FOR EXCELLENCE

"In matters of style, swim with the current; in matters of principle, stand like a rock." (Thomas Jefferson)

Most dictionaries define principles as accepted or professed rules of action or conduct and personal basis of conduct. However, a definition that is more encompassing of a principle is "a fundamental, primary, or general law or truth from which others are derived." We define principles as fundamental facts of life that are in line with natural phenomenon. They are unchangeable with time and season and undeterred by circumstances and situations.

The Second Commandment of God is, "You shall not make for yourself a carved image, or any likeness of anything that is in heaven above, or that is in the earth beneath, or that is in the water under the earth. You shall not bow down to them or serve them." We are called to worship nothing other than the almighty God, which will require us to foster strict principles of excellence.

To worship is to have reverent honour and homage for someone or something that we strongly consider to be sacred. Unfortunately, people without principles of excellence succumb to the gods of today like positions, popularity, prosperity, and sex, drugs and alcohol, the main vices that are destroying people today.

What will eventually make you to become an exceptional leader is nothing other than the principles you foster and the precepts that you adhere to. The first principle that you must recognize is that everything was created for a specific purpose; including human beings, animals, objects and even circumstances. There is no invention without the hand of an inventor, for nothing exists for nothing and nothing happens for nothing.

The principle of purpose, which is actually the foremost characteristics of exceptional leadership, is critical to your success. Purpose is a natural phenomenon that is unchangeable, unhindered by time and season, and undeterred by circumstances and situations.

To attain the level of excellence that would make you to become an exceptional leader, you must make the time to identify a few principles that would guide your decisions and actions. If you require a book that contains all the principles in this world, read the Bible. In fact, the most popular universal principles which cut across time, religion and culture, ethnicity and social status, like love your neighbour as yourself and you reap what you sow, are all biblical principles.

What organizations often name as values are the principles which they use to guide decisions and actions. The dictionary defines values as "important and lasting beliefs or ideals shared by the members of a culture (or organization) about what is good or bad and desirable or undesirable."

Values are meant to influence people's decisions and actions, and not the other way round. How you think, feel and act are reflections of your values. Like principles, your values are the basis upon which you do everything, for they formulate your words and dictate our actions. You must identify the ones you wish to be known for and use them to dictate your action.

What are your principles? Have you ever put yourself through the exercise of choosing a set of principles to guide your life, your career, relationships, business and everything else you are involved in? Over a decade ago, I chose five values that I have consistently used to guide my decisions and actions. They are Faith, Passion, Integrity, Diligence and Fun. Everything I think, do and say is based on these five principles.

Whenever I embark on a project, like the writing of this book, I have to first believe in the concept, the strategies, intent and the content. Our faith in God makes things happen and so is our faith in self and in others, such as you, the readers.

Without a consistent flow of passion, this book would never have been written. And with passion, comes patience and perseverance. A project like this is tedious and could easily be overwhelming, with lots of disappointments along the way. Passion was critical to the successful publication of the book. Our value of integrity demanded that the content be tested, tried and true, and that we do more than enough research to ensure its absolute integrity. We also ensured that credits were given for quotations and references to avoid plagiarism.

My fifth value is the principle of fun, which is something most leaders should set aside time. Fun signifies relaxation. It signifies faith in God, self and others. If you cannot make time for fun, you should not assume a position of authority. Once you discover your purpose in life and make the decision to fulfill it, it will take a toll on your physical, mental and emotional states. This is why I intentionally added fun to my set of guiding principles. Medical researchers have consistently confirmed the significant benefits of fun, laughter and other forms of amusement. Basically, the more you laugh and relax, the longer you live.

According to one online medical journal, which was co-founded by Dr. Jeanne Segal, some of the physical benefits of fun include boosted immunity, lower stress hormones, decreased painful situations, relaxed muscles and reduced chances of heart disease, while some of the mental health benefits include added joy and zest to life, reduced anxiety and fear, relieved stress, improved mood and enhanced resilience.

The journal also stated that the more we laugh and have fun, the more our relationships are strengthened, other people are attracted to us, our teamwork is enhanced, conflicts are defused and groups are bonded. These are the impact of one single principle of fun.

Principles are so critical that it is worth taking the next few hours and even days to ascertain the set of principles that you wish to govern yourself by. If you have never done this exercise before, then start with five or seven values that you wish to be your guiding principles. The first step to ascertain your set of principles is to first identify what you value the most in life, especially when it comes to your relationships with others.

What are the top five to seven things that would make you feel valuable in a relationship? How would you like to be treated by other people? These are your principles, keeping in mind that the standard with which you measure others will be the standard you will be measured by.

SEVEN PRINCIPLES OF EXCEPTIONAL LEADERSHIP

"Important principles may, and must, be inflexible." (Abraham Lincoln)

When executives and entrepreneurs consult with us on leadership development in their organizations, we usually share the following seven principles to guide the decisions and actions of their leaders because they were remarkably obvious in the lives of the exceptional leaders we thoroughly examined.

These Seven Principles of Leadership are not only applicable to those who hold positions of authority, but also to everyone else who desire fulfillment in life. While in no particular order, they are the keys with which you can effectively inform, inspire and influence other people to maximize their potential.

a. **AUTHENTICITY**

"The shortest and surest way to live with honour in the world is to be in reality what we would appear to be." (Socrates)

Authenticity means to be real, trustworthy, reliable and true to self. It means to approach things with no hidden agenda. It is when your decisions and actions are based on what is righteous than what is right, when your mindset is undiluted, uncontaminated and unpolluted. As a leader, what you think, say and do should always be from a pure heart, for the purity of your heart determines the quality of your leadership and relationships. Authenticity requires you to always question your motives—deeply and humbly. It demands that you are open, real and sincere.

The very essence of trust is based on authenticity. Trust is the key to access the potential of others, a significant force that attracts other people to your vision. If you are ever going to gain the confidence of others, if you are ever going to maintain the momentum that is necessary to advance the vision, you are going to need the trust of those whose skills and talents are essential for success. To gain this level of trust, you must be transparent and authentic. You must have a pure heart, with no malicious or selfish intent. You must know and be yourself consistently, for no knowledge whatsoever can surpass that of knowing thyself.

When you ignite your leadership spirit or accept a position of authority, you are vowing to no longer act to satisfy your natural wishes but rather to uplift others. You are making a pledge to be open–minded and kind–hearted. In the words of Stephen Covey, "The more authentic you become, the more genuine in your expression, particularly regarding personal experiences and even self-doubts, the more people can relate to your expression and the safer it makes them feel to express themselves. That expression in turn feeds back on the other person's spirit, and genuine creative empathy takes place, producing new insights and learning." This is what it means to have a pure heart and to be authentic. This is the primary principle of leadership.

As a leader, many people will doubt your motives and question your beliefs, and they will challenge your principles and disregard your opinion. Many people will neither see your vision nor understand your purpose; some will strongly believe that you are motivated by the natural tendencies for popularity, prosperity and power. But what you must absolutely make clear is who you are, what you believe in, where you are going and what you stand for. If others cannot see these in you, they have every reason to question your authenticity.

b. INTEGRITY

"Nothing speaks louder or more powerful than a life of integrity." (Charles Swindoll)

Integrity is the act of standing by what you say and do. As I wrote in my book, *Welcome to Greatness*, "Integrity is the most valuable asset we can ever possess and the most needed companion in our journey en route to fulfillment. It is the highest form of honesty, truthfulness and openness. It is the steadfast adherence to strict moral and ethical principles. It is the unquestionable soundness of moral character. If we must show off anything, then let it be our integrity because no other asset is more valuable."

Integrity is one of the strongest principles that set exceptional leaders apart from the rest, for it requires a high degree of courage, as well as an unwavering commitment to self, others, God, the purpose and vision. In decades of coaching executives, pastors and politicians, this is one principle that they have always expressed a strong desire to improve on. They recognize the importance of it and thus strive to be known for it, especially because the process of leading constantly presents many opportunities throughout the day to either uphold or downplay it.

Integrity is a trait that you either possess or you don't. Unlike faith and passion which may fluctuate according to your state of mind and the situation in which you find yourself, integrity doesn't. You can have faith as small as a mustard seed today and then as solid as a rock tomorrow, and still be considered a man of faith. Integrity is not like that. If you fall short in promises to yourself, others or God, then you lack integrity. In fact, everything you know, say and do will not matter to anyone if you lack integrity. As Zig Ziglar put it, "It is true that integrity alone won't make you a leader, but without integrity you will never be one."

c. GENIALITY

"Nothing is so strong as gentleness, nothing so gentle as real strength." (Saint Francis de Sales)

Geniality is an honourable approach to how you treat others, especially when you are stressed or when they fall short. As a leader, you will always be faced with situations that will challenge your patience and perseverance. You will be confronted with situations that will provoke your thoughts and test your precepts and principles. Despite these, do you remain calm and calculated?

Exceptional leaders are always gentle in their approach with others. This was why Jesus Christ could forgive those who killed Him without cause, why Mahatma Ghandi was able to influence the independence of India without firing a shot, why Martin Luther King Jr. was able to advance his dream of a free and fair America without violence.

Falling short in most of the leadership principles makes your leadership ineffective; however, when you fall short in the principle of geniality, it will gradually turn you into a dictator. Out of all the leadership principles that are known to man, geniality is one of those that directly and instantaneously provoke the emotions of other people.

Geniality is gentleness. And the way you speak to people and treat them directly affects their emotions. If you are gentle with people, they would likely become open to you, and if you are not, they would likely feel hurt, and eventually shut down. When the people who you are meant to cater for are always hurt because of your harshness, your leadership will become ineffective.

Research indicates that information often reaches the emotional part of our brain, which is known as the amygdala, before it reaches the mental part, which is known as the neocortex. This means that when a leader lacks gentleness in his approach to situations and people, he will often impact the emotions of other people negatively, thereby hindering the travel of information from the amygdala to the neocortex. This will further create a communication breakdown, which in turn would cause leadership to be ineffective, if not dictatorial.

This is why exceptional leaders are always gentle. Their geniality is remarkable. Despite their busy schedule and the challenges they have to consistently manage, they always speak the truth in love and have respect for everyone. They recognize that only the strong are gentle, for harshness is weakness.

Gentleness breeds respect, trust and harmony. It will enable you to be more effective in informing, influencing and inspiring others, which is the essence of leadership. Exceptional leaders know this and thus lead themselves accordingly.

In the words of Maya Angelou, the legendary poet, author and writer, "People will forget what you said, people will forget what you did, but people will never forget how you made them feel." To know how gentle you are, you must make those around you to feel comfortable enough to share the truth with you.

d. GENEROSITY

"If you want love and abundance in your life, give it away." (Mark Twain)

Generosity is more than just tossing a dollar into the lap of the less fortunate. It is where a spiritual mindset meets a heart that is so determined to make a difference in the lives of others. As a leader, what you must be generous with the most is your time, for most people are drawn to you to be informed, inspired and influenced, which requires your time.

In the words of Suze Orman, the renowned financial advisor, "True generosity is an offering; given freely and out of pure love. No strings attached. No expectations. Time and love are the most valuable possession you can share." How generous would people say you are with your time, money and even talent?

Exceptional leaders are also known to be generous with their words of encouragement. They understand the power of words and thus use their words to build up people and themselves. Generosity is one of those words that have been relegated to religion alone, even though it is an essential trait for fulfillment in life. Without generosity, leadership is ineffective. As a leader, you must ensure that the quest for growth should never trump the need for generosity.

Exceptional leaders are also generous with their knowledge. It is the same passion with which they sought after knowledge that they also share it. As a leader, one of your objectives must be to ensure those around you know more than you do, without you ever falling behind in the knowledge that is required to advance the vision.

Of what use is your knowledge if those who are attracted to your vision do not leverage it? Millions of people were attracted to the generosity with which the iconic leaders we adore today shared their knowledge. Withholding information that would inform and inspire others is not leadership. No greater honour is there in life than to share with others what was a blessing to you.

e. HUMILITY

"Humility is not thinking less of yourself, it is thinking of yourself less." (C. S. Lewis)

Even though it isn't the first listed, there is no greater principle of leadership than humility, than the ability to be patient and persevere through the most painful of all moments without complaining, blaming anyone or making excuses for your shortcoming.

Humility demands that you are "quick to listen, slow to speak, and slow to getting angry," as the apostle James once advised. If you think you are humble enough, then you are not humble at all, for a humble man wakes up every day with the goal of being humbler than yesterday.

Some dictionaries defined humility as "a feeling of insignificance, inferiority and subservience." This is a misconception, for there is nothing about humility that says you should nail yourself to the cross. Jesus did not drive the nails into His own hands. Did He?

To be humble means to be consistently modest and to not be prideful or arrogant. It is to not consider yourself better than other people, especially when others actually fall short of your standards. It is advisable to feel good about yourself, to think, say and do things that would constantly increase your self-confidence.

It is beneficial to think of ourselves as important, for we all are before almighty God; but we should never think we are more important than other people. This is the height of arrogance, which is the opposite of humility.

Without humility, everything else will fall apart in the 12 Facets of Life that I teach in the School of Greatness: Personality, Leadership, Marriage, Parenting, Spirituality, Relationships, Health & Wellness, Academic Finances, Career, Business and Life in General.

In fact, to learn anything requires you to be humble about what you don't know. This means that until you humble yourself, you cannot learn anything. Without humility, therefore, you will lack knowledge; and without knowledge, people die many times before their actual death.

In essence, humility is the key to unlock the highest level of existence. It is absolutely impossible to successfully navigate through the challenges and complexities of life without humility.

f. HOSPITALITY

"Let not the emphasis of hospitality lie in bed and board; but let truth and love and honour and courtesy flow in all thy deeds." (Ralph Waldo Emerson)

Hospitality is not just an act but an attitude. It is when your concern for others willingly and graciously transcends from a spiritual mindset into their physical wellbeing. When people in positions of authority claim to have an open-door policy, we wonder what other choice they have. Don't you know that the moment that you assume a position of authority or make the ultimate decision to live a life of purpose, you no longer have a door per se?

Of course, you should make the time to relax, meditate and amuse yourself, but the practice of hospitality requires you to be constantly accommodating. As Dr. Myles Munroe consistently demonstrated, exceptional leaders are not just welcoming, but remarkably hospitable, and with open arms.

No story demonstrates love through hospitality than the popular biblical tale of The Good Samaritan. While the biblical story is clear about the honourable authenticity, integrity, geniality, generosity and humility of The Good Samaritan, historical research indicates that Jews and Samaritans hated each other at that time. This means that they were unlikely to help each other, let alone be hospitable in any way. This was likely why the priest and Levite, both of them with positions of authority, crossed to the other side of the street to avoid close contact with the dying man.

Whether you hold a position of authority or not, how hospitable would you consider yourself to be? Would the employees in your company, congregation in your church, students in your school, and friends and family consider you to be accommodating? Are you constantly being The Good Samaritan in your neighbourhood?

For those of you in politics, what are the policies that you must legislate in order to make your country become more hospitable? Hospitality can only be authentic when offered without complaining and grumbling. It is an irrefutable sign of exceptional leadership.

g. **FLEXIBILITY**

"Stay committed to your decisions, but stay flexible in your approach." (Tony Robbins)

This Seventh Principle of Exceptional Leadership is just as critical as the other six principles. Flexibility requires you to have an open mind. The vision, mission, goals and objectives may not be open to discussion, but how we get them executed should be.

Exceptional leaders know that everyone's situation is different and thus makes the time to be well–informed before making decisions and taking action that impact everyone. You cannot be flexible until you fully understand the impact of your decisions.

The corporate and governmental concept of equality, which means to treat everyone equally, may be inflexible depending on the situation. This is why some people and organizations struggle with the concept of diversity. Diversity is the acknowledgement of individual differences for the sake of recognition, appreciation and celebration.

Ignoring the unique characteristics in everyone is the status quo, while acknowledging and celebrating them is diversity. Exceptional leaders recognize that diversity defines the health and wealth of nations—as well as of organizations, and are thus very conscious of it. They seek and seize opportunities to be flexible in order to empower others.

After consulting and speaking on the topic of diversity for many years, I have come to the realization that treating people equally in a diverse workforce may be ignoring their individual differences, thereby leading to inequitable treatment. Therefore, organizations that wish to celebrate diversity must seek to provide equitable treatment for all employees, by moving past equal treatment where differences are ignored, to equitable treatment where differences are recognized, acknowledged and eventually valued. This is flexibility—recognizing that everyone may deserve equal rights, but our method and medium of delivering it must be flexible; otherwise, it is unjust.

If the concept of equality holds you back from accommodating those who are physically or mentally challenged than others in your place of work and worship, then your leadership is ineffective. Successful organizations realize that equity is not just about women and visible minorities, but rather about everyone.

Regardless of our differences, we are all part of a system that depicts the beauty of the world. This is flexibility. It is good to have a made up mind, but a made up mind that is inflexible is made of stone. Principles are rigid and unchangeable; but that is why we have policies. As a leader, you must learn to create policies to perpetuate principles.

While The Seven Principles of Leadership are by no means exhaustive, they are remarkably obvious in the lives of the corporate, political, religious and academic leaders we examined. They are an extension of the set of ten characteristics of exceptional leaders that make up The Leadership Manifesto: Purpose, Principles, Presence, Persistence, Passion, Protection, Prudence, Patience, Perseverance and Prayer. Most of these seven principles may have been relegated to churches only as if they are irrelevant in corporate, school and government leadership, but yet are critical to your personal and professional success.

While integrity may be mentioned in national pledges and among the values of some organizations, including governments and corporations that obviously lack it, authenticity, geniality, generosity, humility, hospitality and flexibility are often left for pastors to preach.

If you wish to position yourself and organization for greater heights, you must become authentic as Jesus Christ, uphold integrity as Martin Luther King Jr., be gentle as Mahatma Ghandi, humble as Nelson Mandela, generous as Mother Teresa and flexible as John F. Kennedy. These are irrefutable principles for exceptional leadership and should be included in your corporate training for organizational success.

3. YOU SHALL HAVE A STRONG PRESENCE FOR INFLUENCE

"The most precious gift we can offer others is our presence. When mindfulness embraces those we love, they will bloom like flowers." (Thích Nhất Hạnh)

Exceptional leaders are always present even when they are absent. Their influence on other people is so strong that even when they are away they are still influential. This would not be so if their presence lacked influence in the first place. A leader that embodies the Ten Commandments of Leadership, while also fostering the Seven Principles of Exceptional Leadership, is bound to be informative, inspirational and influential.

Your presence is more than your physique and profession, more than your aptitude and attitude. It has more to do with your spirituality, the tact and diplomacy with which you approach people and things, the respectable way that you carry yourself consistently.

To have a strong presence of influence, you must first know who you are–your strengths, weaknesses, opportunities and threats, for presence is built on nothing else, but self–discovery, self–awareness and self–actualization. Purpose may provide the destination, passion may generate the momentum, and principles may build the trust, but it is your presence that will determine the direction.

A strong presence of influence is the outcome of the pursuit of wisdom, knowledge and understanding. It is what you possess eventually when you are no longer in doubt of your purpose and when you are willing to do whatever it takes to advance your vision. A strong presence of influence is nothing but a demonstration of absolute faith in yourself, in God and in everyone else.

Nothing will give you a strong presence of influence more than this level of authenticity. When an exceptional leader walks into a room, disorderliness is promptly replaced by orderliness, and profanity will respectfully cease. Does your presence leave such an impression on those in your place of work and worship?

To have a strong presence of influence, you must be purposeful in your approach, be unwilling to compromise your principles, have an unwavering commitment to the vision and constantly developing your capabilities and skills. Those around you must unanimously consider you to be collaborative, cooperative and congruent. In addition, you must be known to "show great aptitude for every kind of learning, well informed, and quick to understand", as Daniel was in the biblical story of the Babylonians.

A leader with a strong presence of influence is not pushy, overbearing or self-seeking. His focus is never on the position, popularity, prosperity, population and power that come with his purpose or position of authority. He is known to be self-confident, to not take things for granted and to not take the name of the Lord in vain, which is the Third Commandment of God.

A strong presence of influence is driven by self-confidence; self-confidence can only be harnessed from within, which is why it is called self-confidence. So quit looking up to people and things for self-confidence, for it is how you see yourself that the world will position you.

Your level of appreciation for others is reflective of your self-confidence. If you wish to increase your self-confidence, increase your level of appreciation for others. Nothing inspires loyalty and support from others more than making them to feel appreciated.

The amount of influence that your presence wields is a reflection of the level of passion that you have for your purpose. Unlike the fear people experience when they are in the presence of dictators, leaders with a strong presence of influence make people feel safe and supported. They make people feel proud and believed in, thus inspiring everyone else to make every effort to advance the vision.

Familiarity may breed contempt, as the old proverb goes, but a strong presence of influence breeds contentment.

4. YOU SHALL BE PERSISTENT FOR PROGRESS

"Persistence is to the character of man as carbon is to steel." (Napoleon Hill)

If you are ever going to accomplish anything worthwhile, arrive at the destination of your desire or make a sustainable impact on humanity, then you must develop persistence. Persistence is the art of proceeding in a predetermined direction gradually, steadfastly, consistently and firmly. Persistence is closely related to perseverance; however, it is more indicative of an unwavering focus, unabashed faith, abounding enthusiasm and an unquenchable desire for success. While to persist is seen, to persevere is felt.

As an exceptional leader, you will be faced with the wind of opposition, the thunder of objection and the flood of oppression. You will be tempted to quit many times over and be enticed by people and things. There will be times when you will question your own purpose in life and begin to doubt the same vision you vowed to die for.

Your closest associates may quit on you and you may even lose everything that you own, including your reputation. Since these things are bound to happen when in the pursuit of your purpose in life, a vision that must be advanced, then the characteristic of persistence is critical. Persistence is reflective of eagerness, enthusiasm, drive and a blunt refusal to back down from what you so strongly believe in. It is one characteristic with many qualities.

The swiftness of lightning, rays of the sun, fright of thunder, persistence of the rain and destructive force of tsunami is incomparable to what will come against you when in the pursuit of your life purpose. Despite them all, the earth is still here. In the same way, you must develop the mindset of persistence and promise to never let your leadership spirit be extinguished, no matter what.

To develop the mindset of persistence requires a firm belief in your vision, in the abilities of other people and in the grace of God. You must believe without a shadow of doubt that only the narrow, rough and rocky road will lead you to the fulfillment you desire. This is the mindset that will inspire you to persist until you succeed. According to Thomas Edison, "Our greatest weakness lies in giving up. The most certain way to succeed is to always try just one more time." Persistence demands that you fix your eyes on the vision.

5. YOU SHALL BE PASSIONATE FOR LIFE

"There is no passion to be found playing small–in settling for a life that is less than the one you are capable of living." (Nelson Mandela)

Passion has been defined in so many ways that most people have no idea what the original meaning is. While some people consider it a powerful or compelling emotion or feeling, as love or hate, internet searches quickly turn up depictions of sensual love, lustful desire and sexual drive.

In all these, it is clear that passion is the outcome of an immovable force, an impenetrable strength, an unquestionable determination and unwavering focus. Passion is what others feel when you are willing to die for a vision you strongly believe in.

Based on its origin, passion has less to do with sex and more to do with stress. Passion may be considered the cure for stress because the strong desire to fulfill your purpose will certainly enable you to overcome the imminent challenges that often causes stress.

According to Abraham Lincoln, "Every man is proud of what he does well; and no man is proud of what he does not do well. With the former, his heart is in his work; and he will do twice as much of it with less fatigue. The latter performs a little imperfectly, looks at it in disgust, turns from it, and imagines himself exceedingly tired. The little he has done comes to nothing, for want of finishing."

Leadership may be a spirit that can only be awakened by purpose and guided by principles, but passion sustains it. Passion enabled Jesus Christ to overcome the suffering associated with His purpose. Passion enabled Nelson Mandela to sit in jail for twenty-seven years in order to fulfill his purpose in life. Passion made Bill Gates to quit his law program in Harvard University to pursue his purpose of creating the personal computer.

Passion made me to quit a well-paying career in the corporate world to pursue my purpose of equipping you and millions of people with this knowledge. Passion, if channelled appropriately, can be an imperative for life and leadership; not just love.

Life is meant to be lived passionately or not lived at all. You cannot complain about everything, blame everyone for everything and make excuses for everything and yet expect to be passionate about life. If you wish to sustain your leadership spirit, you must give birth to your purpose and you will be filled with unquenchable passion.

Above all else, you must consistently exhibit unabashed faith, contagious passion, unwavering integrity, utmost diligence and hearty contentment. According to Zig Ziglar, "When you catch a glimpse of your potential, that's when passion is born."

To generate a consistent flow of passion, you must expand your purpose into a vision. Purpose is what you must fulfill in life for the benefit of humanity, while vision is the magnification of your purpose into a legacy for future generations. An unquestionable determination may enable you to fulfill your purpose in life; however, it is a consistent flow of passion that will guarantee the advancement of your vision.

If your purpose in life is not in line with the vision of the corporation that you are working for, you will be unable to generate a consistent flow of passion. In short, as a body without the spirit is dead, so is vision without passion. Nothing can spur you towards the fulfillment of your purpose and the advancement of your vision more than passion.

Passion is a remarkably strong emotion about something with a positive outcome, not a negative one. If the aim is negative and destructive, it is apathy and not passion. A word that was created to summarize the humble endurance of Jesus Christ as He was unjustly led by tyrants to be crucified cannot be justly used to describe the inhumane acts of terrorists in their unscrupulous attempts to destroy the very freedom for which Christ allowed Himself to be crucified.

As a leader, you owe it to the world to generate a consistent flow of passion to fulfill your purpose in life. You owe it to the world to create the capacity that is necessary for you to be responsive, especially when called upon. You owe it to the world to develop the related skills that you require to become exceptional in your leadership.

You owe it to the world to make yourself available to those who need your support, to live a fulfilled life, to make your life count, and to inspire those around you. This is the peak of human existence, the proof of exceptional leadership, the very essence of life and love.

Contrary to popular belief, passion is neither about bells and whistles, nor is it about sex, drugs and rock and roll; rather, it is about purpose and vision. It is not about being strong and mighty, but rather about the willingness and determination to endure whatever you must go through to advance a worthy vision.

For you to advance your vision, a constant flow of passion is required to keep your leadership spirit ignited. If you must be guilty of anything, let it be of your kindness, of your willingness to die for a greater purpose, of your passion for humanity.

6. YOU SHALL HAVE PROTECTION FOR PEOPLE

"The world will not be destroyed by those who do evil, but by those who watch them without doing anything." (Albert Einstein)

Leaders become exceptional when they decide to stand up for others, to speak up for the rejected and dejected, the downtrodden, oppressed and depressed. None of our Ten Commandments of Leadership compel you to risk your life as much as this; for to be protective of others makes you vulnerable to whatever you are protecting them from.

Exceptional leaders consider this a personal mission, to give up all that they are and have, including their lives, to protect the lives of others, especially those under their care. This is perfectly aligned with our second Organic Law of Leadership, which is the Law of Sacrifice.

A leader who is not willing to protect others, especially those associated with his vision, have given up the right to lead. Of what essence is leading if only to leave your people to face the reproach, ridicule and repercussion from others? Similarly, why marry if unwilling to protect your spouse? What is parenting if unwilling to die for your children?

Why would you want to be a general in the army if only to desert your battalion when the battle gets tougher? Don't you know that leadership requires one hundred percent commitment, which may include your life? In the words of Martin Luther King Jr., "If a man has not discovered something that he will die for, he isn't fit to live." Are you ready for this?

This leadership command to be protective of everyone does not often require you to put your life on the line, except if you are in the military. But it may require you to put everything else on the line, including your position, popularity, prosperity and power. It does not often mean that the lives of your people are in danger, but it may be that their reputation is, or more so, their dignity.

I write this book when terrorist groups are perpetuating despicable acts like never before. While the groups are not worth mentioning in this book, one is known for kidnapping and forcing young girls into sex slavery, another for kidnapping and beheading the expatriates in their countries and another for executing Christians for their faith.

And yet, some countries that claim the presumptuous positions of global leadership are spending more resources to implement highly controversial curriculum on sex–education in junior schools than to protect the victims of these savages. These governments gave up whatever leadership role they may have had by allowing things that matter most to be at the mercy of things that matter least.

Whether a corporate executive, a politician, pastor, professor or professional, you must be protective of everyone and not only those who are in your circle of influence. You owe it to yourself, those who you care for, and even the unborn, to have absolute respect for human lives.

The Sixth Commandment of God, which is to not commit murder, is also akin to the Sixth Commandment of Leadership. The pursuit of purpose and advancement of vision is pointless if you violate this commandment. Most of the leaders who we adore today paid the ultimate price of leadership, namely death, for the sake of others.

We can no longer exempt ourselves from the outcome of our action or inaction which may lead to the death of another, whether we knew of it or not. The fact that whatever we do or do not do could result in the death of another person makes us guilty of murder. When Jesus Christ explained the Sixth Commandment of God about 1,300 years after it was given to the Israelites, He said we are guilty of murder simply be calling another person a fool.

Yet some people continue to call other people fools in their minds, including those who are under their care. Exceptional leaders see persons and not personalities; they recognize the brightness of people's future and not the bleakness of their mistakes. They are committed to protecting people at all costs.

7. YOU SHALL BE PRUDENT FOR EXCEPTIONALISM

"Genius always gives its best at first; prudence, at last." (Seneca)

Prudence is the mother of excellence. It is what must be conceived to give birth to exceptionalism. Of what use is what you do if it lacks integrity and prudence? This seventh commandment is not just what will make you an exceptional leader, but also what differentiates effective leadership from ineffective leadership.

Due to the technological advancement of our time, we are no longer in the era of doing things to the best of our abilities, but rather in the best way possible, and that requires us to develop our abilities. We often remind our children to review their work and then for some reason think we are too good to do the same. A single breach of this commandment could derail your vision.

To be prudent is to always double-check your thoughts, words and actions. It means you do not speak without thinking twice about what is being said, how others may perceive it and why it must be said. It means that while you are decisive, you are dedicated to excellence; while you are not a perfectionist, you strongly believe in excellence.

As a writer, I do not only check the meaning of the words and quotations I use in my books. I do more than what others may consider due diligence to ensure that our knowledge is thoroughly tested and true. Prudence is to go beyond due diligence to what may not be expected of you.

Leaders always have their plate full. They always have multiple priorities that are competing for the top spot. There are always people seeking their advice, opinion and directions. There is the added societal pressure and personal issues they must deal with. Despite this, prudence must never be compromised. It must neither be at the mercy of profit, nor left in the hands of amateurs.

In their quest for profit, some renowned organizations have damaged their global reputation over the recall of products that were hurriedly released to the market without prudence. Even though they claim to have done due diligence, their imprudence resulted in the death of some of their consumers, therefore breaching both the Sixth Commandment, which is to protect everyone, and this Seventh Commandment, which is to always be prudent.

Due diligence is expected of everyone in everything, but prudence is the next level that makes leaders to become exceptional. In the words of Samuel Johnson, the 18th century English poet,

"Prudence is an attitude that keeps life safe, but does not often make it happy."

It is a misconception to confuse diligence for prudence; for where diligence is to accomplish objectives according to exact specifications, prudence is to apply wisdom in everything you do. Due diligence was likely applied in the case of the millions of cars that has been recalled thus far by major automobile companies; however, not prudence.

Cutting corners to save millions of dollars at the risk of other people's lives is despicable, and yet, manufacturers of baby products have been found guilty of this by their governing bodies. These companies later spent more money as reparation than what they would have saved from cutting corners.

8. YOU SHALL BE PATIENT FOR SUCCESS

"Patience is not simply the ability to wait–it is how we behave while we are waiting." (Joyce Meyer)

Bamboo trees are among the fastest–growing plants on earth, with some species growing as much as 35 inches in a day at the rate of 0.00003 km/h, which is approximately one millimeter every two minutes. Even though they are often considered as substitutes for timber, they are not trees but rather a type of grass that belongs to the Gramineae family. This is the fifth–largest plant family and has more than ten thousand species. Due to its legendary approach to growth and sustainability, the Chinese bamboo is the perfect example of the power of patience.

Unlike most trees that grow gradually, the Chinese bamboo does not sprout until its fifth year. Once planted, it must be constantly watered and nurtured for five years before it emerges from the ground. But once it does, it could grow as high as ninety feet tall within six weeks.

It can sometimes grow up to four feet in just one day. Unlike most trees, bamboos can grow on marginal grounds considered unsuitable for agricultural growth. Yet they quickly rise above other trees and plants in the forest.

This is patience at its utmost. It is a virtue essential to the life of each person and an absolute trait of exceptional leaders. Patience allows one to remain calm and calculated especially in the midst of trials and tribulations. Often misconstrued for perseverance, patience is the key to the door of your purpose in life. Absolutely nothing is achieved without patience. If you can't wait for it, it won't come to you.

It takes time to build a solid foundation, to implement efficient processes and procedures, to promote a brand, to effectuate a sustainable change and to advance a vision. Thus, exceptional leaders are persistent in their approach, but patient with its outcome. Like the farmers who cultivate Chinese bamboos, exceptional leaders water their vision every day and nurture those who are committed to advancing the vision, and then wait patiently for the harvest.

Sadly the virtue of patience is underemphasized in our societies today. We are taught from childhood to persist and persevere but we are not taught to be patient for success. We are in an era where we believe things too easily and fall in love too soon. We receive constructive feedback and quickly become defensive. In today's world, corporations demand immediate profits and churches wish to fill their pews in one day. Everyone agrees that patience is a virtue, but no one really understands what patience really is.

If you wish to become an exceptional leader, you must learn to be patient for success. While you do not have to wait for five years to reap the harvest of a cornfield, you may have to wait even longer if you wish to leave a legacy behind. God could have made the universe in a day, but yet he took seven days. He could have made pregnancy to last for only seven days but instead chose nine months.

Nelson Mandela did not have to remain in prison for twenty-seven years, but yet waited patiently for success.

9. YOU SHALL PERSEVERE FOR BREAKTHROUGH

"Many of life's failures are people who did not realize how close they were to success when they gave up." (Thomas Edison)

A simple Google search on the world's greatest failures will turn up the same names of the world's greatest inventors. The search reminds us that we will fail many times before we may succeed. But it is the vision you were born to advance that keeps you trying again and again. In Michael Jordan's words, "I have missed more than nine thousand shots in my career. I have lost almost three hundred games. On twenty-six occasions I have been entrusted to take the game's winning shot, and I missed. I have failed over and over and over again in my life. And that is why I succeed." That is perseverance.

Perseverance is the act of being steadfast in your approach. Even though some people often confuse perseverance with patience, the two are different virtues. While patience is the willingness to wait for a desired outcome, perseverance is the determination to continue despite one's failures and misfortunes. If you are not willing to persevere, you are not willing to lead. In the words of the legendary French poet, Victor Hugo, "Perseverance is the secret of all triumphs."

Henry Ford initially founded and bankrupted two automobile companies before starting Ford Motors in 1903. Albert Einstein, the winner of the Nobel Prize for Physics in 1921, was considered intellectually challenged by his parents and was even asked to withdraw from school by his teacher because of his poor grades.

Walt Disney, the founder of the world-renowned amusement park, failed many times in his business and was often ridiculed by the media. Ludwig van Beethoven's teacher once told him that he was a hopeless composer, yet be became one of the greatest composers because of his perseverance.

Exceptional leaders understand that the journey to advance their vision is rough and tough. So they spend time developing their perseverance ahead of the challenges that lay ahead. They recognize that failure happens to everyone, and persevere in order to better manage and mitigate the impact of it.

How ready are you for the challenges that lay ahead of you? How determined are you to get back up every time life knocks you down? How prepared are you to get back up when life, leadership and love knock you down? How much effort have you put into developing a mindset that will never allow you to give up on your dreams?

Calvin Coolidge articulates it well when he writes, "Nothing in the world can take the place of perseverance. Talent will not; nothing is more common than unsuccessful people with talent. Genius will not; unrewarded genius is almost legendary. Education will not; the world is full of educated derelicts. Perseverance and determination alone are omnipotent."

Exceptional leaders are known for their resilience and tenacity. Are you?

10. YOU SHALL PRAY FOR FULFILLMENT

"Persistence in prayer is a necessity for answered prayers." (Sunday Adelaja)

Exceptional leaders are often self–confident. They consistently strive for self–mastery and are always developing themselves to become better, stronger, wiser and more determined than ever. They surround themselves with special advisers to coach and mentor them in every specific area of their life, especially in leadership. With an unwavering focus and overflowing passion, exceptional leaders are in constant pursuit of their purpose in life, and live lives of principle that are characterized by exemplary patience and perseverance.

Despite adhering to our Leadership Manifesto, exceptional leaders recognize their mortality. They know that while all things are possible, they must be aligned with divine purpose and timing. So they pray always and continually. Your mission and vision can only be possible when it is aligned with your purpose in life and in accord with the divine timing of God. This is why our Tenth Commandment of Leadership is to pray continually, for by prayer we come to learn of God's ways and not our ways.

Prayer is a unique way of communicating our appreciation, supplication, recognition, transgression and transformation to God through our thoughts, words and deeds, with the expectation of receiving divine revelation and rejuvenation. When you pray, thank God for the gift of life and everything you have received and not received. Ask Him for the wisdom to deal with your difficult circumstances. Confess your sins and iniquities and ask God for the strength to live always according to His plan. Finally, ensure that you listen for His response and encouragement through His words in the Bible and the spirit in you.

You are alive at this time because God allowed it. It has more to do with His love and mercy for you than who you are and what you have. Prayer is not about religion but rather about igniting the level of gratitude that would inspire you to become a blessing to others, just as you have being blessed. In the words of John Wesley, the English Theologian, "Prayer is where the action is."

How unfortunate it is that prayers are being banned in schools, governments and public places. How sad it is that many people no longer pray, even for what they obviously have no control over. Regardless of the sophistication of today's technology, the tsunami was still able to claim the lives of about half a million people. Despite the strength of our army and its vast intelligence and enormous abilities, some local terrorist groups are actually winning their wars against nations. Are these not worth praying about?

No single character trait makes a leader exceptional than humility; and nothing demonstrates humility more than prayer. In the words of George Washington, "It is impossible to rightly govern a nation without God and the Bible."

Since the elimination of prayers from school, children have become significantly less exposed to spiritual concepts, including the Seven Principles of Leadership. No wonder we experience the drastic and increasing cases of murder, robbery, rape, assault, drugs, prostitution, arson and many other crimes.

Spirituality is the first of The Seven Organic Laws of Leadership, and prayer is the deepest expression of spirituality. Without prayer, spirituality is inexistent and leadership is ineffective. Prayer enables you to sustain exceptional leadership. It is what would enable you to successfully adhere to The Seven Organic Laws of Leadership. It is the last commandment in The Leadership Manifesto and the key to rest of it.

One of the most popular prayers in the world is The Lord's Prayer, which is a framework that Jesus used to teach His disciples how to pray. Using The Lord's Prayer as a framework, I formulated the following prayer for those in position of authority.

THE LEADER'S PRAYER

Almighty God;

Thank you for enabling me to discover my purpose in life;

Thank you for expanding my mind with such a powerful vision;

May Your declarations and decrees come to pass through the works of my hands.

Bless me with the wisdom and strength to fulfill my purpose and advance the vision.

Endow me with the knowledge and understanding to care for other people around me,

And help me to adhere to The Organic Laws of Leadership and The Leadership Manifesto.

Guide me to not abuse the popularity, prosperity, population and power of my position,

But to recognize your sovereignty in all, through all and over all;

I say this prayer in humility, through Jesus Christ our Lord.

Amen.

THE CONCLUSION OF THE MATTER

These are the Ten Commandments of Leadership, the core of the Leadership Manifesto and the heart of the exceptional leaders we examined. These guidelines will distinguish you in your leadership. They will make you become more effective in your pursuit of purpose and advancement of your vision. If you have come this far in your leadership, you should applaud yourself. According to Stephen Covey, "Principles are guidelines for human conduct that are proven to have enduring, permanent value.

Surely, these have.

Chapter Five

Transformational Leadership

–Five Habits of Exceptional Leaders

"Successful people are simply those with successful habits."
– Brian Tracey

Like characteristics, we are not necessarily born with the abilities that we require to fulfill our purpose in life. And like characteristics, abilities can be learned over time. Everyone was born for a specific purpose and have the talents to achieve the purpose. To be an exceptional leader requires you to develop your natural talents and other potential abilities.

Ability and potential are synonymous, for both of them indicate infinite possibilities. Your characteristics are an indication of who you are, while your abilities are indicative of what you can do. As your ability grows, your character is transformed.

For about two decades, I studied the abilities that enable people to achieve their goals and objectives. I examined the most beneficial abilities inherent to exceptional leaders. It is clear to me that depending on the position of authority you occupy, certain abilities are more instrumental than others. While the gift for public speaking is a beneficial ability for exceptional leadership, it is an absolute imperative for politicians, pastors and professors.

In the same way, the ability of team building is more critical in the role of the corporate executive, pastor and politician than in the role of a professor whose primary duty is to deliver lectures. Many leadership materials often educate readers on the most common leadership abilities, but not many emphasize the ones that you must focus on depending on the position of authority that you occupy. As a result, most leaders are overwhelmed by their attempt to learn leadership abilities, instead of focusing on the ones that are most applicable to their current position of authority.

To master every leadership ability is a daunting task, if not altogether impossible. It is more productive for you to focus on the ones needed to fulfill your purpose in life and advance your vision for humanity. Some leadership abilities are equally critical regardless of your purpose or position. These include effective communication, efficient decision-making, time management, conflict resolution, critical and strategic thinking, coaching and mentoring, work and life balance, budget and finance, team building, and talent management. But I consider these as prerequisites for personal leadership.

FIVE HABITS OF EXCEPTIONAL LEADERS

Since the most important abilities that are required for exceptional leadership alternate depending on the purpose or position of authority you occupy, I decided to ascertain the habits that enable you to focus on the abilities you need to become an exceptional leader. Whether you are a politician, pastor or professor, an executive, entrepreneur or entertainer, the following five habits are essential for your success.

These Five Habits of Exceptional Leaders are essential for anyone who desires a life of purpose and who want to live life to the fullest. They are the habits that will eventually transform your mindset to that of exceptional leadership. These habits encompass many other habits that are required for exceptional leadership, and I found them in the iconic leaders who I studied. Habits determine your success in life; these will initiate your transformation.

1. DELIBERATE PRACTICE

"An ounce of practice is worth more than tons of preaching." (Mahatma Ghandi)

If there is anything you must do as a leader, it is to deliberately practice the characteristics and principles of exceptional leadership. It is to put what you know into practice on a daily basis way more than you talk about them. You may have to take some days off work on vacation, travel extensively for business or leisure, or even fall sick to the point of hospitalization, but as a leader, you are still expected to practice the characteristics and principles of exceptional leadership.

When you are not working on your vision, you should be working on yourself, for exceptional leadership is not a status that you achieve or an award that is given to you, but rather a level of performance that requires deliberate practice. As Lou Holz notes, "Ability is what you are capable of doing. Motivation determines what you do. Attitude determines how well you do it."

Practice is not as beneficial if practicing a skill that you are already exceptional at. The transformation from good to great can only be achieved when you focus your practice on the specific areas or the skill that is hindering your overall greatness. As a keynote speaker, I have to constantly improve my skills, but I cannot claim to do so simply because I speak all the time. I must listen and watch recorded versions of my keynotes to identify the areas needing improvement.

Dr. John Hayes is a cognitive psychology professor at Carnegie Mellon University. For decades, he studied the world's most talented experts and their performances to determine the role that effort, practice and knowledge plays in turning ordinary people to extraordinary experts. He discovered that most of them did not produce their ultimate masterpieces until about ten years into their careers. As such, he concluded that it takes an average of ten years to master a skill.

Other research supported Dr. Haye's conclusion and further suggested that even the most talented people usually achieve global status only after a minimum of ten years or ten thousand hours of deliberate practice. This makes patience, which is the eighth commandment in our Leadership Manifesto, even more critical in leadership. It does not mean that you cannot become an expert in less than ten years, but rather that you must deliberately and diligently put in the required time for you to become exceptional in leadership. As the old adage goes, "Practice makes perfect."

The term "deliberate practice" was coined by Dr. K. Anders Ericsson, a Swedish–born psychologist at the Florida State University. He used the term to indicate the immerse benefit of how you practice versus how many times you practice. His research indicated that it is more beneficial to breakdown the characteristic or capability which you wish to develop into parts, and then focus on the parts that require improvement the most, while ensuring that your performances are constantly measured and constructive feedback is always obtained.

In retrospect, to become exceptional in leadership requires you to first identify the specific skill that you must improve on and the abilities that you require to be exceptional in your purpose or position. Then break down that identified characteristic or ability into steps before working on the specific parts that require improvement.

The decision to improve on your communication is a honourable one. But is it on your listening skill, public speaking, eye contact, writing, body language or one of the many other components of communication? This is the role that deliberate practice has in the acquisition of expert performance.

2. STRATEGIC PLANNING

"Plans are nothing; planning is everything." (Dwight D. Eisenhower)

Nothing is more foresighted than strategic planning, than clearly putting on paper what you wish to actualize tomorrow. This is one of the most critical capabilities of exceptional leadership. Planning is the skilful act of identifying and tactfully documenting what must be said and done periodically to achieve a predetermined objective.

The only guarantee that you are going in the right direction in life, leadership and love is if your plans are in perfect harmony with the divine purpose that you were created for.

Otherwise, you are not.

While mere planning is the tactful deliberation over how to achieve a specific objective, strategic planning is a more elaborate process whereby the priorities for a long period of time are set, resources that are required to execute the goals and objectives are measured, the outcomes forecasted, ways to sustain profitable growth are devised, and whatever must be done to ensure the advancement of the vision are clearly documented. Strategic planning takes into account the human capital required to advance the vision for the specific period of time, as well as the Key Success Factors (KSF) to measure performance.

To become exceptional in leadership, you no longer have the luxury of doing things for their own sake. You can no longer afford to think of only today. If you are ever going to become exceptional in leadership, you must become strategic in your approach. At any point in time, you must be able to share a three to five and even seven to ten year strategic plan to advance your vision.

In the words of American author Alan Lakein, "Planning is bringing the future into the present so that you can do something about it now." Do you have a strategic plan for your vision?

A strategic plan is a series of manoeuvres that successfully advance a strategic vision. A strategic plan includes:

- A Vision Statement that articulates the final objective when it is all said and done;
- A Mission Statement which states what you are striving to accomplish and how you intend to do so;
- Articulated Goals that identify major milestones along the way;
- Objectives, the things that must be done in order to achieve the goals;
- And Corporate Values, namely, the guiding principles that must guide all decisions and actions of the organization.

To ensure the continual advancement of your vision, your strategic plan must also include:

- A SWOT Analysis, which is an in-depth review of your Strengths, Weaknesses, Opportunities and Threats;
- The Competitive Advantages, which are what sets you apart from similar groups;
- Key Success Factors (KSF), which are metrics that will indicate continual success;
- Key Performance Indicators (KPI), which are objective ways to measure operational and financial performances as well as the physical, mental emotional and spiritual wellbeing of all who are engaged in your organization's success.

As Winston Churchill puts it, "However beautiful the strategy, you should occasionally look at the results."

3. FOCUSED PRIORITY

"The key is not to prioritize what's on your schedule, but to schedule your priorities." (Stephen Covey)

In this age of heightened distraction and overwhelming information, maintaining focus is a predominant challenge. Leaders as swamped like never before as they make every effort to cope with multiple priorities all at the same time; in fact, the tasks of some projects and initiatives make some executives consider them all as top priority. This is a blatant disregard for the definition of priority.

The mere fact that some things are important does not mean they must all be done at the same time. Even God took his time to create the universe. Whether it was actually seven calendar days or not, we know everything wasn't created at once.

A priority is something that must precede other actions in order to achieve the final goal. Nothing can precede a top priority, which is why you cannot have multiple top priorities. There are multiple priorities but one ultimate priority, which makes the skilful act of focused priority one of the habits of exceptional leaders.

If you wish to become exceptional in leadership, you must promptly identify the most important task of an overall project. The key to focused priority is "no." It is your ability to say no to everyone and everything else that is bound to derail your focus from what truly matters, including yourself and desires.

For you to be exceptional in identifying what is a priority requires you to be proficient in needs–assessment, decision–making and relationship management. It requires you to know what truly matters, the courage to make everything else secondary and the confidence to manage the relationships that may be impacted by what gets postponed.

Until you are able to decide what you must do and when you must do it, everything else you do may not matter. When focus becomes a habit of yours, you will always be aware of the abilities that you must develop to achieve your vision. Focus reveals opportunities to develop yourself, to advance your vision and to fulfill your purpose. In fact, focus establishes your priorities.

When faced with multiple priorities that must be done at the same time, you must go back to your vision, purpose and plan. You must determine which of these competing priorities aligns the most with the vision. Then you determine which of them agrees with your purpose the most, which advocates your principles and values the most and finally, which enables people to maximize their talents the most. These will enable you to identify your priorities.

Exceptional leaders have processes and procedures in place to manage the influx of activities and opportunities. With an effective team in place, they are usually not faced with tactical decisions or involved with daily routine. When there is macro involvement in operations, their focus is on strategic planning.

Unfortunately many leaders claim that they do not have time for their personal development, team building, peer mentoring, corporate awareness and social responsibilities, despite these being priorities of exceptional leaders. If you do not schedule these priorities, your leadership will soon become ineffective.

You may take another break from reading this book to prepare your list of outstanding activities and assess each one of them on their urgency and importance. If important and urgent, it should be done by now, so get to it right away. If considered urgent but not important, move it to the bottom.

4. STRATEGIC PARTNERSHIP

"Alone we can do so little. Together, we can do so much." (Helen Keller)

The lack of confidence that some people in positions of authority have in their associates makes many leaders to assume tasks that should be delegated or outsourced. One habit of exceptional leaders is to build strategic partnership with people who they can learn from and do things with in mutually–benefitting ways. Attempting to advance your vision all by yourself is counterproductive, if not arrogant.

You can cultivate strategic partnerships with those who are working directly with you to advance your vision, or with those who are advancing a similar vision in a different capacity. Exceptional leaders also create strategic partnerships with those who wish to learn from them through coaching and mentoring, with their clients, citizens, congregations or students, where appropriate.

Exceptional leaders recognize that while they may act alone, they should never travel alone and cannot succeed alone. They seek opportunities for strategic partnership to maximize their resources. Have you identified those who you should partner with to bridge the gaps in your abilities?

While your purpose is meant for you to fulfill on your own, the advancement of your vision requires you to build strategic partnerships with those whose purpose is tied to your vision, as well as those whose vision definitely intersects with yours.

Regardless of the purpose you were created to fulfill or the vision you are determined to advance, it is part of your destiny to be directly involved in the development of others. In the words of Ken Blanchard, "None of us is as smart as all of us." This is why exceptional leaders seek strategic partnership with others.

If some leaders and organizations would only be open to this concept-strategic partnership, their impact and income would remarkably increase. In the pursuit of purpose, partnership and collaboration are critical components of success.

Strategic Partnership is a concept that churches should consider if those in positions of authority wish to become exceptional in leadership. We have seen too many churches in the same neighbourhood being led by pastors who are exceptional in praise and worship and barely good enough in preaching and teaching. If you are exceptional in praise and worship, why don't you merge your small congregation with another whose pastor is exceptional in preaching and teaching so that you may take charge of the praise and worship for the larger congregation?

Don't you know that this will enable both of you to become exceptional leaders in your own rights, demonstrate the unity that Jesus Christ often preached about and magnify the impact and income of the ministry? What is wrong with two or more congregations joining their Christmas banquets together to provide more opportunities for their congregation to fellowship and even save resources in doing so?

The natural tendency for a particular position has created in many people the desire to be the CEO of their own organization. Organizations such as Walmart understand the power of this concept and have formed many strategic partnerships and alliances with other organizations to ensure their mutual success. If you are heading the same direction with someone else, why not work and walk together to keep each other company along the way?

5. CONSISTENT PRODUCTIVITY

"Productivity is never an accident. It is always the result of a commitment to excellence, intelligent planning, and focused effort." (Paul J. Meyer)

The very essence of leadership is to produce, to generate results, to advance a vision, and to inspire others to discover and fulfill their purpose in life. This is productivity. It is what Peter Drucker, the Management Consultant guru, defines as "the balance between all factors of production that will give the greatest output for the smallest effort."

Many leaders give tremendous time towards their vision to the detriment of their health and wealth. They sadly experience little or few results. Whereas exceptional leaders put in lesser time than most leaders do and achieve astronomical results. Why is this so? How productive do you consider yourself to be?

According to Investopedia, "factors of production" is "an economic term to describe the inputs that are used in the production of goods or services in the attempt to make an economic profit. The factors of production include land, labour, capital and entrepreneurship."

Based on my research on the lives of exceptional leaders, their factors of production are nothing other than The Seven Organic Laws of Leadership that we wrote about in Chapter 3. They are Spirituality, Sacrifice, Strategy, Service, Substance, Success and Succession. These are keys to maximum productivity.

You must build the habit of productivity to become an exceptional leader. One of the key indicators of productivity is knowledge. It is how much you know of how much you need to know that will determine how much you succeed. This is why leaders are learners.

You can only be productive when you put in the required amount of time and effort, and initiatives are executed according to a strategic plan. It is not what you start that matters, but what you finish. What you start is only temporal, while what you finish is completed. Exceptional leaders are known to finish whatever they start.

I discovered in my research that productivity is hindered the most by procrastination. I learned that it is not often what leaders don't have that impedes their progress, but rather what they don't do. It is not the lack of resources that hold then back, as they often believe, but rather, it is their lack of resourcefulness. Because of this habit of consistent productivity, exceptional leaders set goals and do not back down until they are accomplished. They believe that only what is measured can be managed and implement statistical reporting.

Productivity is not just about producing widgets and making profit. Rather, productivity transcends effectiveness and efficiency to encompass the mental and emotional states of people. How employees, congregation and students feel after work, worship and study respectively have a stronger impact on the productivity of your organization than what is perceived.

According to Remi Dairo, Africa's foremost consultant and speaker on productivity, "Beyond skills and knowledge of staff, there are intrinsic variables that provoke organization productivity. Much more than systems and processes, the emotions and feelings of employees have proven to be of great factor for performance."

Dairo coined the term "affective productivity" which he defined as "the approach where the process of input and output take into cognizance the emotions and feelings of the people within the process of production and the consumers alike in order to increase performance and excellent delivery."

As an exceptional leader, your strategic plan should include Key Performance Indicators to measure your organizational progress, as well as the affective productivity of your organization. You should also have a Leadership Scorecard in place to measure your effectiveness as a leader.

Organizations that have an elaborate performance measurement system in place are widely known to be more productive than those that don't. Rather than using seniority, performance measurement systems would make governments to be as productive as corporations. Even in churches, pastors should implement ways of measuring productivity.

MEASURES OF TRANSFORMATION

Habits are the fundamental reason for success or failure. To be an exceptional leader requires you to practice these five habits every day until they become part of you. It requires you to be consistent in them and make them part of your personal and corporate culture. If you wish to be productive, you must deliberately practice the habits that are required for success: always make strategic plans, always focus on priorities and always consider strategic partnership at every opportunity.

It is the deliberate practice of these habits that would eventually lead to transformational leadership. They are bound to usher you into higher levels of exceptionalism and set you apart from leaders who are overwhelmed by their quests to master every leadership capability. Before retiring for the day, always ask yourself the following questions:

- Have I deliberately practiced my skills today?
- Have I adhered to my strategic plan?
- Did I focus on my priorities?
- Did I nurture my strategic partnerships?
- Was I as productive as I could be?

Write down your responses and ensure to acknowledge your accomplishments for the day and what must be promptly done the next day. This is how you turn abilities into habits that would eventually result in transformational leadership.

Malcolm Gladwell, the American author said it best: "Transformation isn't about improving. It's about re–thinking."

The time to do so is now.

Section Three

The Process of Leading Exceptionally

As a leader, you will always hear many things. You will always feel, do, say and learn many things. But it is what you remember at the time you should that makes you exceptional.

Chapter Six

What Leaders Often Forget

–Five Priorities of Exceptional Leaders

> "Be faithful to that which exists nowhere but in yourself – and thus make yourself indispensable"
> – Andre Gide

A very important skill that makes leadership exceptional is that of remembering. It is the ability to remember things when you should, how you should and why you should. Without a retentive memory, your leadership will gradually become ineffective. In fact, memory is the bridge that separates effective leadership from ineffective leadership. Most leaders actually know what to do to become more effective, but they often forget what they know when they need to remember it the most.

To be an exceptional leader requires you to turn your memory into a powerhouse that generates knowledge consistently and promptly. These are two effective ways to respectively maximize your mind and heart, and to explore your subconscious being. The more things you remember, the more effective your leadership will become. The more things you forget, the more ineffective your leadership. In the words of American author James Caroll, "Forgetfulness is the handmaiden of tyranny."

As a leader, you will always hear many things. You will always feel, do and say many things. But it is what you remember at the time that makes you exceptional. As a leader, you will always hear many things. You will always feel, do, say and learn many things. But it is what you remember at the time you should that makes you exceptional. Simple things such as remembering the names of the people who you work with, and even the names of their family members who they are fond of the most, go a long way to boost their morale and respect.

Leveraging technology and hiring an executive assistant may help you with remembering, but often not how or why you should remember things. Your Blackberry device may remind you of a lunch meeting with some investors and the agenda of the meeting, but not about their personalities and diets, which are the things that would make them feel important.

While you are not expected to remember everything, you are expected to remember what matters most in the sphere of your leadership. You are expected to always remember your purpose, vision and mission statements. You are expected to remember your goals, objectives, targets, decisions, timelines, promises and the influx of information that people in authority must manage on a daily basis. To become an exceptional leader, therefore, requires you to have an effective way of receiving, managing and disseminating information, which is where leadership capabilities meet management skills.

The ability to remember your knowledge and responsibilities must be deliberately practiced with ardour, for exceptional leaders are known for exceptional memories. They leave nothing to chance and maximize the technology and techniques of remembering things. Some are known to read aloud to themselves because it is a proven technique of storing information in memory. Imagine a pilot who is about to land a plane, but doesn't remember how to do so safely. This is the type of dire situation that some leaders find themselves. They attended seminars and read many books about conflict resolution, but are unable to remember how to resolve conflicts when they are faced with one.

How well are you able to remember the things that matter most? If it is lower than what is required, your leadership will gradually become ineffective. Of what use is reading this book if you cannot remember what you have learned when it is needed the most? How unproductive it is to undergo a rigorous strategic planning session with your partners only to forget the outcome and your action items?

As human beings, we are prone to forgetfulness. But to forget certain things in life have sometimes resulted in death. This is why exceptional leaders are known to consistently sharpen their focus. In the words of the American author Samuel Butler, "Memory and forgetfulness are as life and death to one another. To live is to remember and to remember is to live. To die is to forget and to forget is to die."

To harness the power of remembering, we strongly recommend that you discipline yourself enough to wake up early in the morning. Exceptional leaders are usually awake by 5 A.M. to sharpen their mental capability. The early hours of the morning are usually the most mentally productive time of the day. It is when our brainpower is at its best. It is highly recommended that you spend some quiet time with yourself and with God.

I spend time with God by reading the scriptures, followed by a brief praise and worship song to refresh my soul and fervent prayers to rejuvenate my spirit. This is seamlessly followed by a moment of reflection, which is the act of recalling things from my memory for the purpose of contemplating and deliberating on their urgency and importance.

I conclude this highly productive habit by writing down what I learned and my plans for the day in my journal. This is when I make note of the most powerful thoughts and ideas that I received during my meditation and reflection. In the words of Robin Sharma, a Canadian author and professional speaker, "Writing in a journal reminds you of your goals and of your learning in life. It offers a place where you can hold a deliberate, thoughtful conversation with yourself." After completing these spiritual, mental and emotional exercises, I engage in physical exercise before I shower and take the day on with vigour.

Based on decades of training, coaching and mentoring leaders worldwide in developing their skills of focus and remembering, I identified the top five things that leaders often forget. These five things would make leaders exceptional only if they would remember. The Five Things Leaders Often Forget is actually one of my most requested keynotes for leadership conferences because it exposes leaders to their blind spots, and equips them with strategies to bridge detrimental gaps which were created by our natural tendency of forgetfulness.

Remembering these five things on a daily basis will, in turn, enable you to remember other pertinent information that would eventually help transform you into an exceptional leader.

FIVE THINGS LEADERS OFTEN FORGET

1. PERSONAL DEVELOPMENT

"An unexamined life is not worth living." (Socrates)

Personal development is the life–long gradual process of learning principles and precepts for the sole purpose of becoming an exceptional leader and living a fulfilled life.

Personal development is a mindset and a way of being. It is also a lifestyle of intentionally developing the main elements of your existence: physical, mental, emotional and spiritual. Personal development is the daily, deliberate and lifelong determination to enhance your mind, energize your body, and excite your spirit while also inspiring and empowering others daily to do the same as well.

Until you are willing to invest in yourself, you are not ready to progress in life. Without regularly putting in substantial time and effort into your own personal development, you won't be developing yourself enough to manage and mitigate the ever–increasing challenges of leadership. No other activity will enable you to become exceptional in leadership more than personal development.

Many leaders develop themselves consistently while vying for higher positions of authority and then make no more effort after they are in the desired role. This is counterproductive, for if you achieved your current level of success based on your knowledge, nothing else will enable you to achieve the next level more than increased knowledge.

Are you one of those leaders who forget to develop themselves because of the busyness of their schedule? Do you make time to attend seminars and read books that would enable you to develop your capacity and capabilities? Do you have a coach and mentors for key areas of your life?

Bill Gates is the richest person on the planet and he is still an avid reader. He makes time for personal development like never before and still seeks advice from others to improve on his leadership. What about you?

2. TEAM DEVELOPMENT

"A mentor is someone who sees more talent and ability within you than you see in yourself, and helps bring it out of you." (Bob Proctor)

Bringing a group of people to work together on a vision is one of the most tedious tasks known to humanity; and yet, many leaders often forget to develop their team after forming it. They are so focused on projects and profits that they forget to develop those who execute the goals and objectives. Don't you know that if your profit is growing faster than your people, then your profit is unsustainable?

We have seen too many leaders pressure their employees and yet offer no team development. Forming the team may have been tedious, but developing them is essential, or else they will operate ineffectively and inefficiently for as long as possible before eventually falling apart completely. A part of being an exceptional leader requires you to consistently develop your team.

Team development is not just a series of activities to get more out of people. Instead, team development includes activities deliberately orchestrated for the purpose of enabling people to achieve self-discovery, self-awareness and self-actualization. Team development activities ought to be educating, empowering, enriching, energizing and encouraging.

The most effective team development or team building activities are subtly woven into the day-to-day operations and not those periodic activities that can be checked off the calendar of events. Exceptional leaders recognize the power of developing their teams and they include these activities into their strategic plans.

Exceptional leaders put in the necessary effort to ensure that as they pursue personal development, they encourage their teams to do the same. They cultivate an environment and infrastructure to ensure that every one grows. In fact, the budget of an exceptional leader is considered incomplete until a significant portion of it is directed towards team development. In the words of Richard Branson, "Train people well enough so they can leave, and treat them well enough so they don't want to."

Dr. Bruce Tuckman, a psychologist who graduated from Princeton University in the 1960s, performed an extensive research on the theory of group dynamics. It is a theory that examines how people think and act within social groups. In 1965, he suggested that there are four stages of group development, which he called, Forming, Storming, Norming and Performing.

In 1977, Tuckman added a fifth stage called Adjourning. According to Tuckman, every activity in the lifetime of any team falls into one of these five phases. Forming is the first phase, which is where the group is formed and are introduced to the vision, mission, values, goals and objectives, as well as the collective Strengths, Weaknesses, Opportunities and Threats (SWOT).

Storming is the second phase where team members get to learn about each other and make effort to build cohesion and synergy, while Norming is the third phase where team members assume responsibilities for their individual roles and the collective efforts to advance the vision. Performing is the fourth phase where constant productivity is expected since team members are expected to have gained competence and maturity by this time. Finally, the fifth phase is Adjourning. This is where the team would complete the task that they were formed to execute and breakup if necessary.

Exceptional leaders know that these five phases can only function effectively if the team members are being developed consistently throughout the process. As a leader, you can form, storm, norm and perform all you want, but sustainable success is dependent on team development. You must set aside the time and resources that would enable your team members to constantly develop their abilities or you will certainly have to Adjourn, per Tuckman's concept. But this time, prematurely.

3. PEER DEVELOPMENT

"Feedback is the breakfast of champions." (Ken Blanchard)

Peer development is one of the five things leaders most often forget. Some leaders are known to develop themselves and their teams, but not many summon the courage to develop their peers. Even though it is beneficial, they withhold constructive feedback from their peers because of the fear of reproach.

In one of my speaking engagements, where I delivered this message to some executives in a major financial institution, some participants admitted to being aware of their peers' weaknesses, but felt it wasn't their place to advise their peers accordingly. Every time you miss an opportunity to develop, coach and mentor your peer, you are hindering maximum productivity in your organization.

Mentoring is the deliberate sharing of your experience with another person. Typically, the mentor is older than the mentee in experience and often in age too. As an executive coach and keynote speaker, I mentor fellow coaches and speakers worldwide. I also have a mentor. In fact, grounded in my passion to equip everyone everywhere with coaching and public speaking abilities, I formed mentoring groups for coaches and speakers who are less experienced in these fields of work.

This is Peer Development—a systematic way for peers to collaborate and cooperate on mutually-benefitting learning objectives. If you are unable to receive constructive feedback from your peers, you are not fit to lead.

Mentoring is critical to leadership, and must not be forgotten. Without mentoring, you violate the Seven Organic Laws of Leadership, and in particular, the seventh one, the Law of Succession. Mentoring is one of the most effective ways to identify and confirm potential successors, while peer mentoring is a deliberate two-way program with a mutual agreement to grow together, support one another and watch out for each other.

If you do not establish a network of peer mentors to refine each other's ideas, to help you see what you may have missed, to encourage you to manage your challenges and frustrations, and keep you in check where required, you will gradually move yourself from being stressed to the dangerous state of distress. In addition, your leadership will become ineffective before gradually becoming dictatorial.

Dr. Myles Munroe was a renowned advocate of mentoring. He often talked about five men who he subjected himself to their authority even though they had no formal authority over him. According to him, these five men could question his authority at any time and even sought the opinions of his wife, children and associates regarding his life and leadership without first seeking his permission to do so. In the words of King Solomon, "The way of fools seems right to them, but the wise listen to advice."

Who advises you on matters that you claim to matter?

Whether you are a sole proprietor, the CEO of a corporation, the senior pastor of a church, or the president of a nation, you need the input of a peer. If you wish to become an exceptional leader, you must identify at least one person who has consistently demonstrated the level of exceptionalism that you are aiming for, just as I identified Dr. Myles Munroe. It was the desire for peer development that led me to him, which eventually gave birth to the publication of this book. You will be amazed at the impact of peer development when you humbly open yourself to it.

4. CORPORATE DEVELOPMENT

"Unless you try to do something beyond what you have already mastered, you will never grow." (Ralph Waldo Emerson)

Due to the increased demands placed on leaders, many leaders have limited their knowledge, activities and efforts to the specific areas of their roles and responsibilities. They focus on their individual and departmental goals and objectives without relating them back to their corporate objectives. They usually know what to do to improve their abilities and capacities, but have no idea about what the organization must do in order improve its overall capabilities and capacity.

Exceptional leaders are fully aware of what is going on in their organizations. Exceptional leadership fosters a spirit of corporate development well beyond what they are paid for. The least paid and influential employee in an organization who desires to become an exceptional leader must make it his business to know how well the organization is progressing versus its potential, targets and competitors.

Corporate development is a series of activities that enable the growth of an organization. While it must be a priority for the senior executives in every organization, it must also be a major concern for everyone else, especially those who have ignited their leadership spirit.

Some of the activities that usually fall under corporate development include strategic alliances, mergers and acquisitions, introduction and elimination of products and services, divesting of assets and divisions and even recruitment of management teams. As a principle, it is the will and ability to do all these to the extent of your knowledge, regardless of your position in the organization.

Exceptional leaders move beyond merely doing things to the best of their abilities to doing things the best way possible. They consider corporate development as a culture and not a concept. They willingly perform corporate development activities without even know it. With an unwavering focus on whatever is required to advance the vision, exceptional leaders thrive in both what they are paid and not paid to do. This is a trait of successful organizations whereby everyone does everything possible in support of corporate development.

5. COMMUNITY DEVELOPMENT

"The only thing that will redeem humanity is cooperation." (Bertrand Russell)

Regardless of the purpose and vision of exceptional leaders, they are always known for community development. They always advocate for the less–privileged and support initiatives that protect people, animals and environment. Exceptional leaders know that to succeed, the communities they serve must succeed as well.

Despite their busyness and focus, therefore, they are committed to community development. They make time to network with people in their communities, seizing every opportunity to meet the needs of the less–privileged, while challenging those who are more privileged to be and do more.

The United Nations defined community development as "a process where community members come together to take collective action and generate solutions to common problems." This broad term categorizes the activities of leaders within our communities who are committed to the advancement of the people within the community.

While some people are hired by government agencies and organizations to manage community development activities, it is everyone's responsibility, particularly those who have ignited their leadership spirit and hold positions of authority. Some leaders are so focused on advancing their vision that they often forget to participate in community development.

You mustn't.

Despite the differences in the agendas of a corporation and the communities it operates in, there are many opportunities for collaboration. In fact, an organization that is not involved in community development is not fit to operate in any community. How can you explain extracting and refining petroleum products in a community that lacks basic human amenities?

Community development could be about building infrastructures, improving the awareness of people regarding policies and available programs and amenities and providing health care and education. All of these activities belong to the realm of community development.

I vividly remember visiting a top executive in a major global corporation, in a popular city in Africa, and was appalled at the dilapidated road that led to his multimillion-dollar home; even more horrifying were the number of prestigious cars in his garage. Based on his riches, it would have cost him nothing to build and support his community. Exceptional leaders would jump at opportunities such as these.

This is one of the main reasons why many parts of Africa are underdeveloped. Most people in the developing nations turn to their governments for community development. However, community development is not simply the task of governments. Rather, we all have a responsibility for community development. Governments may build community centres for recreation and relaxation, but there is nothing wrong with members of the community volunteering to ensure they are not dilapidated.

The government may build schools, but there is nothing wrong with the corporations and churches in those areas offering the necessary resources to ensure the schools' success. This is by no means absolving governments from their responsibilities, but rather advocating the acts of individual and social responsibilities. What is life if not to expend it for others?

An exceptional leader who has consistently demonstrated the habit of community development is Dr. Anthony Sterling. A dentist in

Brampton, Ontario, Canada, Dr. Sterling is widely known for leading the way in numerous initiatives to support youth, new immigrants and women. He even organizes his own community events, such as his widely attended summer BBQ, to foster unity and harmony among the diverse groups in his community.

At the book launch for *Welcome to Greatness* in 2011, I announced our Inside Out Transformation initiative that was designed to donate copies of our books to detention centres and shelters of abused youth and women around the country. During the event, Dr. Sterling came to me quietly and offered to sponsor 200 copies for the youth detention centre in his community. He asked for the books to be shipped to his office so he may write words of encouragement in every copy before they were delivered to the youth at the detention centre.

While leaders may often forget these five things, they are indicative of what you must do to become an exceptional leader. You must develop the habit of remembering them in order to remain an exceptional leader. With this framework in mind, which of them do you need to improve on the most? What is your plan to do so?

The sequence in which they are outlined is more logical, even though they are in no particular order. Without consistency in personal development, leadership as a whole will soon become ineffective. If you are not developing yourself, you cannot develop your team and neither would you have the courage to mentor your peer.

Chapter Seven

Culture of Exceptional Leadership

–An Impetus for Organizational Success

> "Lack of culture means what it has always meant: ignoble civilization and therefore imminent downfall."
> – Frank Lloyd Wright

Like many words in this day and age, the true meaning of culture has been diluted over time. There are so many myths to debunk and misconceptions to unravel. In fact, as far back as 1952, a book on culture written by two anthropologists, Clyde Kluckhohn and Arthur Kroeber, identified over one hundred and fifty definitions of culture. Their research identified the sheer complexity of the term. But it is absolutely necessary that we understand culture, for culture is what forms our thoughts and behaviours.

Your culture is your overall outlook on life. It is the way you have been conditioned over a long period of time to see things. While it is often inherited, it is more often reflective of what you are exposed to, whether you agree with it or not.

Culture represents the value system that you were brought up in, coupled with the behaviours and beliefs you were exposed to and the ideas and knowledge you gathered over time. Culture is strongly influenced by many things, particularly ethnicity, religion and socio-economic status. As Thomas Carlyle, the Scottish Historian, once said, "Culture is the process by which a person becomes all that they were created capable of being."

ORIGINAL PURPOSE OF CULTURE

"Wisdom deals with causes and origins." (Aristotle)

Before proceeding, therefore, it is wise to reveal the origin and meaning of culture. Culture derives from a term used by the ancient Roman orator Cicero in his *Tusculanae Disputationes*. Written out of the enormous pain he experienced at the death of his daughter, the *Tusculanae Disputationes* is a series of five books. In them, he made a reference to 'cultura animi', as an agricultural metaphor for human culture. While it was used to insinuate the "cultivation of the soul," the word is closely related to 'cultivate', which is to promote, enhance or improve the development or growth of plants with utmost care and dedication.

Throughout the centuries, the meaning gradually shifted to include the development of people with utmost care and dedication. Today, everything is naively considered 'culture,' for the term is now used to summarize prevailing beliefs, ideas, images, perspectives, attitudes and opinions, whether they promote, enhance or improve the development of anything or not.

To summarize as culture, the illegal use of drugs, the misuse of great inventions like technology, and the abuse of people simply because they are different in one way, shape or form, is an absolute misconception. This is because these ideas and actions, regardless of how prevailing they may be, do not promote, enhance or improve the development or growth of anything.

From its original meaning, therefore, it is clear that culture is an atmosphere that is filled with characteristics that foster and cultivate the development and growth of people. With the purpose of advancing a grander vision, culture energizes the body, empowers the mind and enriches the soul. It is assertive and affirmative, firm and focused.

Culture promotes and progresses and does not retrogress. It is the outcome of the utmost dedication that a group has for the advancement of a vision. According to Mahatma Gandhi, "A nation's culture resides in the hearts and in the soul of its people." Culture is bound to advance human beings and not destroy them.

IMPACT OF ORGANIZATIONAL CULTURE

"Culture eats strategy for breakfast." (Peter Drucker)

Based on the original meaning of culture, many organizations have none. Only a few corporations, governments and churches can boast of a place of work or worship that consistently promotes, enhances and improves the growth and development of their people. Even worse is the fact that many schools have no culture as well. They can claim to have what is commonly referred to as pop culture, but if it fails to effectuate development or growth in the lives of their students, then it is chaos and confusion, not culture. If the true meaning of culture was upheld in our societies today, the rate of crime would be decreasing rather than increasing.

The default state in the world today is that of self. What many people care about these days are their wishes, wants and desires. We buy things we don't need, are easily swayed by popular opinions and claim to love the neighbours who we have not met. You cannot grow when all you think and care about is you. With this prevailing attitude, culture is gradually becoming extinct. This perspective is gradually suppressing true culture by moving the world from sacrifice to sacrilege, purpose to pleasure, service to disservice and purity to profanity.

The quest to produce more, have more, say more, see more, eat more, sleep more, do more and be more is so rampant that most places of work and worship are becoming like drive-through outlets and fast-food restaurants. It is the culture of these restaurants to be focused on fast-paced, fast-turnaround and quick-delivery, for it advances their vision. While we hope their employees are developing and growing as fast as they deliver the food, building relationships with their clients is not part of their culture. The focus of their employees is to serve their clients as fast as possible because it advances the vision of fast-food restaurants. Many things may contribute towards the success of an organization, but success can be sustained by nothing else, but culture; true culture that fosters growth.

An organization that has culture progressively develops its population and advances its vision, for culture is meant to support the advancement of a vision and not the other way round. When culture is inexistent, confusion is rampant, chaos is inevitable and the vision will gradually and eventually die. This is the world we live in today, the very reason why God said that "people perish for the lack of vision."

By virtue of its true meaning, culture is growth, and growth is leadership, for it compels people to stretch themselves to support a greater purpose and vision that would impact humanity. Culture compels people to be different from what is popular, and challenges them to make a difference.

If the ideas, beliefs, values and knowledge that constitute the shared bases of the norm in your organization do not foster the development of its population, culture is inexistent. No home or organization has a stronger foundation than that which is built on a positive, progressive and productive culture.

The culture of an organization may evolve with time, but the original meaning and purpose of culture is unchangeable. Culture is meant to support the growth and development of things and not to destroy people and things. If the culture a society or organization claims to have is not advancing a progressive vision for humanity, it is false. Just as the growth and development of a plant requires utmost care and dedication, so does the growth and development of a vision and the population it attracts require utmost care and dedication.

Culture is not something that is left to chance or that happens haphazardly; rather, it must be built intentionally and systematically. Like a gardener would cultivate his flowers, so are leaders expected to cultivate in their places of work and worship, The Seven Organic Laws of Leadership, The Seven Principles of Exceptional Leaders and The Leadership Manifesto.

FIVE STEPS TO CULTIVATE LEADERSHIP CULTURE

"The only thing of real importance that leaders do is to create and manage culture." (Edgar Schein)

Since the concept of culture is so diluted, I developed a framework to enable you to cultivate a leadership culture in your home, corporation, church, school and organization. It is based on my in–depth research on this topic and the real experiences gleaned from the diverse types of organizations that have consulted with me over the years. For this framework to actually work, those in positions of authority must first embrace The Seven Organic Laws of Leadership, The Seven Principles of Leaders and The Leadership Manifesto.

Leadership culture is an outcome and not a mandate. It is when those in positions of authority foster an environment that enables people to increase their capabilities, feel self-worthy and utilize their talents. It is when people are equipped, energized and encouraged to do more than what is being asked of them and give more than what is being received. It is the result of gladly deferring the praise of accomplishments to your people and willingly assuming the blame and responsibility for whatever goes wrong under your leadership.

Leadership culture is reflected in an atmosphere where the leadership spirits of the people in your organization are in constant harmony with their entrepreneurial spirits to advance the vision. It is when those in positions of authority have been able to inform, inspire and influence others to ignite their individual leadership spirit. It is a place of work or worship where everyone is an ambassador, whether they hold positions of authority or not.

1. EDUCATE YOUR POPULATION

"Education is the most powerful weapon which you can use to change the world." (Nelson Mandela)

A common misconception about education is that it is a series of classes which a person must take at specific institutions of learning. Instead, education is the intentional sharing of the knowledge required for the advancement of a specific purpose.

The type of education that you should offer must be clear and focused. It must be to inform those entrusted to you of what leadership is, to inspire them to develop their minds and influence them to demonstrate their skills. You may adopt this leadership curriculum, which I developed out of this book and include modules such as The Seven Organic Laws of Leadership, The Seven Principles of Leadership and The Leadership Manifesto. With education often comes examination, whether formal or informal. Train and test your teams formally and informally. Without applicable knowledge, there is no leadership, and culture is inexistent.

If what you claim to have learned is not obviously reflective in your way of being, then you have learned nothing at all. Everyone in your organization must be able to state the vision of the organization or else your leadership is ineffective. It you desire success in life and in your organization, then education must be a recurring item on the agenda of all meetings and the only item that should be allowed to go over budget. As President Nelson Mandela once said, "Education is the most powerful tool you can use to change the world." Above all else, education is the most powerful tool to change people's mindset and build culture in your organization.

2. EMPOWER YOUR POPULATION

"Leaders become great, not because of their power, but because of their ability to empower others." (John C. Maxwell)

Leadership culture demands that you always provide your population with opportunities to practice what they learn. Equipping people with leadership abilities and not providing them with opportunities to demonstrate leadership is an absolute waste of time and money. Leadership culture is one where employees, students and congregations are consistently encouraged to take initiatives, to step up and to step out. In an organization with leadership culture, mistakes are not allowed, as long as the lessons are learned.

There are millions of books on the topic of empowerment, illustrating its importance in life, leadership and love. People do not perform more than their level of empowerment. The performance of employees is usually in direct proportion to the expectations of those in positions of authority. In the words of John C. Maxwell, "Leaders are great not because of their power, but because of their ability to empower others." Empowerment is the foundation upon which leadership culture is built. It is what determines if you have leadership culture.

Empowerment is to authorize, approve, sanction, enable, encourage, delegate and permit others to take charge, with trust, patience and grace. It is to strategically prepare people for what they doubt in themselves and tactfully inspire them to proceed accordingly.

Leadership culture demands that you consistently raise the bar and allow people to make mistakes without the fear of retribution, as long as they learn from their mistakes. Empowerment is less about words and more about action; it is one thing to say mistakes are allowed in your home and organization and quite another to have the reputation of someone who lacks trust, patience and grace.

To empower others effectively, you must be authentic in your approach, maintain integrity at all times, be gentle in all your ways, and generous with your time and resources. Empowerment of those around you is so critical that you should not leave your home each day without creative ways to do just that. In the same way, you should not leave your place of work and worship until everyone around you is empowered.

3. ENRICH YOUR PEOPLE

"No man can become rich without himself enriching others." (Andrew Carnegie)

It is a misconception to confuse enrichment with empowerment, for enrichment is a much deeper experience. While empowerment provides your population with opportunities to demonstrate their leadership capabilities, enrichment lavishes them with whatever is required to seize those opportunities. While empowerment has a philosophical undertone, enrichment has a spiritual undertone.

It is one thing to tell people that they can achieve a goal, which is encouragement, and quite another to teach them how to do so, which is education. However, enrichment provides your teams with whatever is required to achieve the goal.

Successful organizations know what is required for their population to succeed and thus make the necessary provisions without delay. Regardless of how educated and empowered your population is, if you are unable to provide them with the tools and techniques they require to excel at work, your organization lacks culture.

Enrichment is a holistic approach that includes all aspects of life: physical, financial, moral, mental, emotional and spiritual. The people who are enriched feel elevated and endowed. They cannot help but share their enrichment with those in their circle of influence. This is another critical component to cultivating leadership culture.

4. ENERGIZE YOUR POPULATION

"No company, small or large, can win over the long run without energized employees who believe in the mission and understand how to achieve it." (Jack Welch)

This is where motivation comes in.

Motivational activities gear people up and inspire them beyond their wildest dreams. One of the most effective ways to energize your population is to celebrate their successes, to acknowledge their personal achievements as well as their professional ones.

Bonuses are great, but surveys indicate that employees value quality times with their executives over postcards and plaques. In the words of Theodore Roosevelt, "Nobody cares how much you know, until they know how much you care."

Some corporations overwork their employees, while many churches over–teach their congregations. Jesus Christ still made time to attend weddings and to feast at the homes of those who were not even His followers. So what excuse do you have for not creating atmospheres of fun to energize those in your home and places of work and worship?

Exceptional leaders recognize the power of motivation, and therefore use it to increase the productivity of their population. When people are energized, they can achieve way beyond their own expectations; so why not energize your population on a consistent basis?

As a leader, never be oblivious to the efforts of your population, even if not achieving the desire objectives. Never postpone activities that would increase their trust in you and confidence in the vision you are leading. These are opportunities to inspire and motivate them. People must know that you believe in them, are willing to support them through their challenges and that you appreciate their efforts to advance the vision.

5. ENCOURAGE YOUR POPULATION

"Encouragement is oxygen for the soul." (John C. Maxwell)

Encouragement is one of those concepts that are gradually becoming extinct in corporations, schools, government and even the churches. In my previous book *Welcome to Greatness*, I dedicated an entire chapter to the concept of encouragement because of its importance. I wrote, "while we would agree that we could use a regular dose of encouragement from the people around us, most of us hardly receive any–and most likely, hardly give any either. And of course, we blame this "oversight" on our busyness, lack of time, and forgetfulness; when in fact, many of us are simply just not making enough effort to encourage those around us."

Exceptional leaders are always fostering cultures that encourage people to step out in faith, to discover their purpose in life, to pursue their passion and to face their fears and challenges confidently. The most effective way to change behaviours and cultures is to model it for others and then encourage them to follow suit. Dare to rename one–on–one meetings with your population to Sessions of Encouragement and you will ignite a leadership culture at its best. In the words of Richard Branson, "When you lavish praise on people, they flourish. Criticize, and they shrivel up."

There is nothing wrong with sharing constructive feedback with people. In fact, it is your responsibility as a leader to do so. However, exceptional leaders have a way of delivering feedback to make others accept it with humility. Exceptional leaders are encouragers. Perhaps you should learn to always offer two encouraging message of feedback to your employees for every constructive feedback offered.

HOW TO SUSTAIN LEADERSHIP CULTURE

"Hope is not a strategy." (Rick Page)

To cultivate and sustain a leadership culture in your organization may require a committee of employees that is a balanced mix of those in positions of authority and those who are not. Their objective should be to thoroughly review this framework and identify the quick ways in which this can be implemented promptly in your organization.

The committee should develop a roadmap that should outline the initiatives that must be executed to build and sustain leadership culture in the organization. This plan must have specific timelines and periodic checkpoints and reviews indicated as well. It should outline how The Seven Organic Laws of Leadership can be exemplified consistently in your organization.

This will be a major paradigm shift for your organization, and must, therefore, be treated delicately and as a priority. The committee should also review all human resource policies, processes and procedures to ensure that they promote the leadership culture that is being built in the organization. Interviewers should be trained to place more focus on leadership abilities, even above academic qualifications.

Bonuses and other reward programs should be reengineered to promote leadership abilities like personal–development, initiatives, ownership and acts of fiduciary duties and social responsibility. In the words of Jim Collins, "You absolutely must have the discipline not to hire until you find the right people." This is why your corporate strategy must include how to ensure the continual cultivation of leadership culture in your organization.

"The way things have always been done here" must be closely examined to ensure the mindset of everyone in your organization should be that of leadership, entrepreneurship and ownership. Every component of culture, including the prevailing beliefs, ideas, images, perspectives, attitudes and opinions, must be reviewed by the committee to ensure that what people see, hear and talk about is part of the leadership culture that the organization is cultivating.

Even more importantly, the values of your organization must be reviewed, and The Seven Principles of Leadership—Authenticity, Integrity, Gentility, Generosity, Humility, Hospitality and Flexibility incorporated. These are critical components of a positive, progressive and productive organizational culture.

These principles will undoubtedly create an atmosphere where people constantly encourage one another, where they educate, equip and enrich themselves with the knowledge, skills and awareness that are required to maximize their potential. This should be the focus of your Organizational Culture Committee. They must constantly come up with ways to sustain it and beware of traditions that counteract it.

In the words of Edward S. Casey, "The very word culture meant 'place tilled' in Middle English, and the same word goes back to Latin *colere*, 'to inhabit, care for, till, worship'. To be cultural and to have a culture is to inhabit a place sufficiently intensely to cultivate it–to be responsible for it, to respond to it, to attend to it caringly." This is what is required to cultivate leadership culture.

The key success factor of your leadership and, indeed, your organization as a whole, is not your vision. It is not even your mission or passion; but rather, it is the culture of your organization. We learned that regardless of your words and actions, beliefs are what determine outcomes. Even when the outcomes are not reflective of beliefs, beliefs are so strong that they can still turn things around.

The truth of the matter is, above all else, culture wins. If the prevailing beliefs in your corporation, church, community, college and government are not in support of a vision that advances humanity, you violate the Law of Success. This is why we have formulated the following pledge as a Declaration of Exceptional Leadership.

A pledge is a solemn promise of what you intend to do or refrain from doing in order to achieve a set objective. It is to foster a leadership culture in your organization. We recommend that everyone in your organization, especially those in positions of authority, make this pledge with you. It is even advisable to form accountability groups to meet periodically to mentor each other along the way.

While I have more instructions in the afterword on how to maximize this book and other programs I have in place to sustain your exceptional leadership, making this pledge is a recommended first step. Since accountability is a critical component of leadership, ensure to make the pledge with at least one other person present. Dr. Myles Munroe had five accountability partners, and so do I.

In the words of Bob Proctor, "Accountability is the glue that ties commitment to results"

LEADERSHIP PLEDGE

A Declaration of Exceptional Leadership

My name is _____.

I pledge to adhere to The Seven Organic Laws of Leadership, The Leadership Manifesto and The Seven Principles of Exceptional Leadership, as outlined in *The Mystique of Leadership*.

I am committed to be spiritual in my mindset, to be sacrificial without boundaries, serving without expectations and strategic in my approach.

I shall make every effort to consistently be a leader of substance and use the Succession Planning Framework in *The Mystique of Leadership* to nurture successors that will advance the vision.

I shall not dwell in my position of authority or engage in the pursuit of popularity, prosperity and power.

I shall not be swayed by the population or by popular culture that is not in line with both the moral compass that leadership is meant to be and the vision that I am committed to lead.

I am committed to living a purpose–driven life all the days of my life, and will constantly inspire everyone else to live a life of purpose.

I promise to neither abuse my influence nor misuse my affluence and shall make every effort to adhere to The Ten Commandments of Exceptional Leadership in *The Mystique of Leadership*.

I am committed to the constant development of the related capabilities that will position me and my organization for massive success. The successful advancement of the vision shall always be my focus.

When I fall, I shall stand. When I struggle, I shall seek advice. When I am in distress, no one else will feel it.

I promise to equip myself, empower my team, encourage my peers, energize my organization and exhilarate my community; and I shall remember to be responsible, responsive and resilient until the end.

So help me God.

Afterword

–Next Step to Greatness

> "Strength and growth comes only through continuous efforts and struggle."
> –Napoleon Hill

Congratulations for completing this rigorous journey on how to become an exceptional leader!

Applaud yourself for having gone through this intense framework and for your determination to be an exceptional leader. While I hope that you stopped along the way to practice some of the strategies you learned in it, it is now time to demonstrate the principles and philosophies in the best way possible and on a daily basis. It is now time to incorporate the concepts and precepts into your daily life so that your employees, students and congregation may emulate you and build a leadership culture in your corporation, school and church.

Acquiring the knowledge was necessary. Even more necessary, however, is the implementation of the knowledge you acquired. This is why we have formed a Mastermind Alliance called Eximious, which is a Latin word for selected, distinguished, eminent, excellent and of course, exceptional.

Eximious, therefore, is a group of leaders like you who are exceptionally determined to keep their leadership spirit alive. It is made up of corporate executives, politicians, pastors, professors and other professionals such as athletes, coaches, lawyers, doctors and likeminded leaders who would like to participate in the type of strategic partnerships that I discussed extensively in this book.

Since you have thoroughly read this book, I would like to assign you to an Executive Coach who will work with you on the gaps in your own leadership that must be bridged. This will enable you become an exceptional leader.

Your first session with an Executive Coach is valued at $499, but will be complimentary for reading through this book. Subsequent sessions would be gladly offered at a significant discount.

As you learned in the book, everyone needs a coach and mentor, so why not allow us to work with you to sustain your exceptional leadership? All you have to do to receive this free gift is register at www.alexihama.com and then book your complimentary session.

Upon completing the registration process, you will receive a link to download a welcome message from me. In this video message, I will elaborate on some of the concepts in this book while also laying out a master plan for you to sustain exceptionalism in your leadership. I will also let you know how you can get your leadership questions answered, and how to get in touch with the members of Eximious closest to you, regardless of your country.

Our vision is to have chapters of Eximious in every country around the world. That way, the combined wealth of knowledge will be maximized by those who wish to run the race with perseverance. If you wish to host a chapter in your city, corporation, church or college, please send an email to alex@alexihama.com.

Leadership is neither a profession nor a position; it is neither a job nor a job title. Rather, it is a lifelong journey of personal development. Completing this book, therefore, is only the beginning of the next level of your journey to greater heights and another exciting part in your pursuit of purpose and the advancement of your vision.

Nothing truly ends, for every ending is a new beginning. I urge you to book your complimentary session so that you may develop a master plan for your continual progress in exceptional leadership. Don't forget this.

Contact us if you would like to implement *The Mystique of Leadership* as a curriculum in your corporation, church, government, college or organization, and to order copies of the book in bulk to initiate leadership culture in your population. Contact us too if you would like us to deliver parts of this book as a keynotes or workshops.

Simply send an email to alex@alexihama.com with your curriculum, bulk order, and presentation requests.

This is a leadership revolution and I welcome you to it with the hope that you will seize the opportunity to partner with us and spread it around the world. In the words of Abraham Lincoln, "The best way to predict the future is to create it." Let us work with you to create one for yourself and organization.

Welcome to Greatness!

Acknowledgement

–Vote of Thanks

> "No duty is more urgent than
> that of returning thanks."
> –James Allen

Writing a book of this magnitude is a daunting task and can only be achieved through the cooperation and collaboration of many dedicated people who so strongly believe in the dire need for exceptional leadership in corporations, communities, churches, colleges and governments. Therefore, words and space are insufficient for me to express my appreciation to all of you who stood by us before, during and even after the publication of this book.

First and foremost, I hereby express my hearty appreciation to Dr. Myles Munroe of blessed memory, for expanding my vision beyond frontiers to the shores of countries that I did not even know existed. Your belief in me, Papa Myles, coupled with the honourable way that you adopted me as a son, mentee, friend and brother, still makes me feel blessed beyond measure. This is why we dedicate this book as a tribute to you, for inspiring it in me. Rest in peace with your wife of noble character, Lady Ruth Munroe, with whom you departed this world.

I would like to thank those who have taken time to train, coach and mentor me over the years. These people have consistently demonstrated the very principles that this book promotes: Carmen Puzzo, Archbishop Margaret Benson-Idahosa, Rev. Gordon Constantine, Bishop (Dr.)

Kingsley Osayande, Bishop Innocent Ordu, Pastor Sue Kiteley, Rich Worthington and Bishop (Dr.) David Kings. I would also like to express deep appreciation to Rev (Dr.) Bernice King for sharing with me firsthand information about her father, Rev (Dr.) Martin Luther King Jr. May God Almighty bless all of you and continue to expand your work to the glory of His name. Amen.

To my outstanding team of reviewers, researchers, endorsers and those who played key roles throughout the project: Dr. Sam Chand, Anthony Ndulue, Professor Iyorwuese Hagher, Dr. Bruce Cook, Silvia Jordan, Greg Ihama, Pastor Sunday Adelaja, Catherine Gardner, Charles Ezomo, Barrister Kingsley Jesuorobo, Dr. Yvonne Oswald, Dr. Pepe Ramnath, Emmanuel Dei-Tumi, Amos Dada (Ph.D.), Dr. Stacy LeMay, Pastor Ghandi Olaoye, Dr. CB Peter Morgan and a host of others all over the world.

I express my deep and heartfelt appreciation to my special editor, Don Beyers, for his magic with words, belief in the philosophies of this book and partnership in faith and leadership. I honour you and appreciate the strategic advice that you and everyone else provided to make this book exceptional and successful.

To my immediate and extended family for the consistency of their amazing support: My dad and mom, Barrister and Mrs. Tony and Mary Ogbeide-Ihama, who are exceptional leaders in their own rights; my brother and sister, Don Osa Ogbeide-Ihama and Dr. (Mrs.) Faith Iwu; My beloved biological and adopted children, Brandie, Travis, Naomi, Luc and Dylan; and my darling wife, best friend, special adviser, amazing lover, and number one fan and supporter, Onanon Samantha Ihama. My love for all of you is immeasurable.

Finally, I would like to express our wholehearted appreciation to our God Almighty, the Creator of Heaven and Earth and Exceptional Leader of the Universe. What a great honour to have been a messenger of this message in a time that it is needed the most. Thank you, Father, for supplying the strength to continue when I felt weak, the tenacity to forge ahead in the face of opposition and the resilience to complete the work despite the so many challenges along the way. Thank you for the example of exceptional leadership that You showed us through Jesus Christ, our LORD, Saviour and Master.

May You pave the way for *The Mystique of Leadership* to transform the lives of millions of people around the world. Amen.

Special Tribute to Dr. Myles & Ruth Munroe

– By Bishop David Oyedepo

Living Faith Church Worldwide

Myles and I called ourselves 'twin brothers'
Myles, my twin brother is gone up to glory
Ruth, his partner in life and death has gone to eternal rest
Faith and I miss you both!

Our moments together on this side of the Jordan were most memorable. We stayed together on several occasions under the same roof. We lodged in same hotels time and again; we shared the platform together preaching the good news of the Kingdom over the years. Our friendship of over 24 years was a most enriching and adventurous one. Our partnership in ministry was also a most profitable and rejuvenating one.

Myles, my twin brother
A bundle of inspiration
A man of spiritual depth and insight
A leader of leaders and teacher of teachers

Ruth, a bundle of joy and divine radiance
Your smiles were ever contagious,
You exhumed gentleness, love and care like a fountain
You were indeed a priceless jewel!

The two of you were swifter than eagles
You literally traversed the globe
As you taught nations the principles of the Kingdom
You were both as strong as the unicorn,
Energetic, untiring, never relenting, purposeful and focused

I could still remember how Myles and I took all the inaugural induction lectures for the pioneer faculty and staff of Covenant University in August 2002. All of Myles' meetings on our church platform were ever inspiring and impactful. The Living Faith Church Worldwide really misses you!

Good night Myles, my twin brother!
Good night Ruth, his partner in life and in death.

About Alex Ihama

Alex Ihama is an internationally acclaimed speaker who has been delivering keynotes on leadership and strategy to a variety of audiences all over the world for almost two decades. Widely known for his contagious passion, he is often sought after by executives, politicians, pastors, entrepreneurs, academicians and other groups for the extensive knowledge which he acquired from his dramatic childhood, his deep research on life, spiritual and business matters, his wide intercontinental travels and his consistent involvement in literally thousands of lives through speaking, coaching, consulting, training, mentoring and writing.

With academic and experiential background in Personal Proficiency, Leadership Development, Corporate Strategy, Project and Relationship Management, Sales, Team Building, Diversity, Youth Engagement and Community development, coupled with the numerous leadership positions he held in reputable organizations, including two of Canada's largest banks, Alex's messages transcend religious, cultural, racial and socio-economic backgrounds. According to the CEO of one of North America's largest banks, "Alex manages a fine line of being inspirational, provocative, humorous, passionate and purely entertaining."

His book, *Welcome to Greatness*, which was published by Balboa Press, a division of Hay House Publishers, the publisher of globally renowned authors like Dr. Wayne Dyers and Marianne Williamson, has received praises from global leadership experts such as Dr. Myles Munroe. Based on the principles of this book, he founded and presides over the School of Greatness Worldwide, a unique educational institution that offers free webinars and seminars on life skills that are not taught in conventional schools, yet required to excel in life after school.

Alex is also the founder and executive director of three organizations, including a non-profit arm which partners with corporations, churches, communities, schools and associations to donate inspirational books to detention centres and youth and women shelters across Canada and worldwide. From Peru to Portugal, Singapore to Switzerland, United States of America to United Arab Emirates, and Nigeria to Nicaragua, Alex's keynotes, inspirational articles, tireless social media activities, and regular radio and TV appearances have been classified as nothing but "captivating, challenging and compelling."

His vision is simply to "Make You Think Deeply, Act Passionate and Grow Steadily."

About Alex Ihama International

Alex Ihama International is a global firm of professional speakers, coaches, consultants, trainers and mentors who partner with corporations, schools, communities, churches and governments around the world to build the abilities and capacities that these organizations requires to achieve stringent goals and objectives.

Both Alex Ihama International and our School of Greatness Worldwide are subsidiaries of Welcome to Greatness Inc., which is registered in Ontario, Canada and in some countries around the world. Our shared goal is to be the Constant Catalysts for Change (C^3) in corporations, communities, churches, colleges and governments all over the world.

School of Greatness Worldwide is a unique educational institution that uses seminars and webinars to facilitate classes on life matters, leadership, entrepreneurship, public speaking, coaching and more. The first of its kind worldwide, this school uses a robust technological infrastructure to educate students on life, entrepreneurial, leadership and topics that are not taught in conventional schools, but yet required for success in every area of life.

VISION STATEMENT

A Renewed Mind for Everyone

MISSION STATEMENT

To Consistently Make You Think Deeply, Act Passionately and Grow Steadily through Speaking Engagements, Coaching Sessions, Consulting Services, Training Workshops and Mentoring Programs.

CORE SERVICES

In support for our vision of A Renewed Mind for Everyone, we have carefully developed five Core Competencies over the last two decades. These have become the Core Services through which we remain the Constant Catalysts for Change (C^3) in corporations, communities, churches, colleges and governments. They are as follows:

1. **SPEAKING**

    We deliver inspirational keynotes that empower people to access higher levels of their potential for greater impact, based on years of our intense psychological, physiological, spiritual and philosophical researches on human behaviour, peak performance and maximum living. While walking a fine line of being provocative, humorous, passionate and purely entertaining, participants are complimented and challenged in the same sentence, and depart with no alternative but to fall into a deep assessment of self & sense of pride.

2. **COACHING**

    We provide the Life, Business and Executive Coaching that people need to overcome the character and situational challenges that are hindering their personal and professional success. Whether face-to-face, by phone, email or other form of technology, our coaches take pride in the absolute transparency and diligence they bring to each and every coaching session. Our holistic approach, coupled with the depth of our coaching methodology, enables our clients to make sustainable changes to their own amazement.

3. **CONSULTING**

We consult with corporations, schools, communities, churches and governments around the world on variety of challenges and opportunities, while working with management and executives on how to maximize the human potential and resources of their organization. Whether on how to build a leadership culture, implement strategic people, process and technology changes, or manage multi-million dollars projects and initiatives, we enable the effectiveness and efficiency to sustain the Return-On-Investment (ROI).

4. **TRAINING**

We facilitate rigorous short and long-term training programs in support of organizational vision and strategic initiatives. Whether it is to make leadership more effective, increase sales, expand marketing efforts through innovations like social media or maximize diversity, our training programs are known to equip people with the tact and techniques to be, do and have more in life. Our holistic approach to training enables us to make participants more aware of their strengths and weaknesses that they were unaware of.

5. **MENTORING**

We offer one-on-one and group mentoring programs to thousands of people worldwide, with most of them being participants at our events, followers on social media and referrals from those who have been impacted by our programs and products over the years. In addition to our different categories, we have an Executive Coaching Club, designed for high-level corporate executives and global entrepreneurs to mentor each other on strategic opportunities, while going through our Executive Leadership Program.

VALUE ADDED OFFERS

- To enable their continual development, participants in our speaking and coaching engagements are registered for a lifetime mentorship program in our School of Greatness.
- To encourage participation at our speaking engagements, copies of Alex Ihama's books are distributed to some active participants while coaching programs are raffled out.
- To ensure suitability of our training and consulting services, a 3 to 5 year support and follow-up plan are offered to organizations upon the successful execution of initiatives.
- To support the organizations we partner with, we offer their employees, congregations and students personalized Personal Development Program (PDP) that grants them confidential access to our robust suite of training, coaching and mentoring programs, and discounts for their direct and extended families.

FEEDBACK ABOUT ALEX IHAMA

Alex Ihama is one of the most dynamic and engaging speakers in Canada today. The opportunity of hearing him speak will reveal many things about Mr. Ihama to the listener, and should not be missed. His messages, and the poise with which he delivers them, will at once inform the listener that he is very knowledgeable about the topics that he chooses to expound on. However, not only is he knowledgeable, he is also very insightful and thoughtful in his delivery. These traits are very useful for helping the listener to easily put Mr. Ihama's messages in perspective. Mr. Ihama has a very smooth and easy way of providing very relevant topics in an engaging manner. The result is that his audience is held spellbound. His most powerful tool, however, is the entertaining manner in which he delivers his messages. As a result,

Alex is highly effective in connecting with his audience, because while they are paying attention to his wit and humour, before they know it, they will have learned something from him. **(DR ANTHONY STERLING, PRESIDENT/CEO, STERLING DENTAL)**

Alex is a talented and passionate enabler in helping people/groups to "join the dots". He consistently demonstrates unmatched energy and commitment to goal achievement. **(MARK HART, VICE PRESIDENT, COMMERCIAL MORTGAGES, CANADIAN IMPERIAL BANK OF COMMERCE (CIBC))**

Alex's public speaking and presentation skills were strong. No matter what the content, his presentations always were engaging, interactive and dynamic. You always sensed that people in the audience were interested in what he had to say and that interest seemed to carry throughout the entire speaking engagement. **(RICHARD RAMEZ, SENIOR DIRECTOR, CANADIAN IMPERIAL BANK OF COMMERCE (CIBC))**

Alex is a tireless worker in cultivating the success of others, personally and professionally. He has an inspiring message that sparks individuals, to be the best possible versions of themselves. His message of greatness is tied to both civic and individual responsibility. While he motivates others, his life matches his doctrine, as he strives to give to others globally. Alex is a tremendous example of a man that ignores 'human limitations' and works tirelessly to help others do the same. **(ROWAN BARRETT, EXECUTIVE VICE PRESIDENT, CANADA BASKETBALL)**

I was truly looking forward to hearing Alex Ihama and his keynote address. I did not know what to expect, but I was struck by his presence, enthusiasm and the electricity he brought to the room. He walks and manages a fine line of being inspirational, provocative, humourous, passionate and purely entertaining. His experiences and wisdom are evident in his remarks. He compliments you and challenges you in the same sentence. He takes you on a journey of emotions which invokes laughter, deep thinking, reflection, and pride, and leaves you wanting more. **(MARK CUMMINGS, PRESIDENT/CEO, SCOTIA BANK LIFE INSURANCE COMPANY)**

Alex Ihama is a force that is engaging, passionate, spiritual and powerful. Once you are in his presence you will be totally mesmerized by his zest for life. I am amazed by his compelling spirit to help others actualize their God-given gift, and the unique "Star" that lies in the depths of their being, waiting for the right opportunity to shine outwardly. Thank God for blessing our planet with Alex, as he has been the 'opportunity' for many. I appeal to all those who have been searching for self-actualization, power, purpose and greatness to give yourself another chance by purchasing Alex's book, "Welcome to Greatness". If you have bought one of his books already, purchase another one for a family member, friend or a young person who is on that 'Search'. This is a life-changing opportunity and an unforgettable experience. Thanks Alex, for your commitment to humanity and community, changing lives one day at a time across the globe, with your gift to all. **(PAULINE CHRISTINE, PRESIDENT, BLACK BUSINESS AND PROFESSIONAL ASSOCIATION (BBPA))**

Alex Ihama's speech to the audience could not have been a more poignant reminder that success is a journey, not a destination. While we are inspired by the achievement of these distinguished men, I felt uplifted by Alex's plea that we must keep moving forward, and we must reach greater heights. Few speakers are imbued with an ability to discharge a seemingly weighty message with earnest while, at the same time, delivering levity and laughter with precision. **(MARLON REID, VICE PRESIDENT, TORONTO DOMINION (TD) BANK)**

Alex is an excellent communicator who speaks with passion and wisdom. His words as a coach are select and powerful and he can take anyone willing to listen and act, from zero to hero. **(OMEY SAMAROO, SENIOR MANAGER, MONERIS SOLUTIONS)**

Alex is a coach of the highest integrity, and is thus a model of the ICF Code of Ethics. In addition, he has a sharp mind and kind heart, which allow him to effectively establish trust and intimacy, create awareness, design creative and high-impact developmental actions for his clients and manage progress and accountability. This is based on his tireless commitment to the welfare of others and his passion for learning. **(LESLIE WILLIAMS, PRESIDENT, LEADERSHIFT CONSULTING)**

Alex brings a high level of commitment, talent, diligence and compassion to his coaching work and his preparation and follow-up of his in-session work. He blends rigour with intuition, and is able to maintain a strong presence with his clients. Alex significantly contributed to the clients he worked with during our program. **(ANNE WRIGHT, PRESIDENT, ANNE WRIGHT & ASSOCIATES)**

The delivery style of Alex's speech is extremely engaging, with his tone changing to make people take notice! His messages were clear . . . we all own our success and we are accountable. He made relevant references, used himself as an example and asked the listeners for understanding. **(JUDY RYELAND, DIRECTOR, CANADIAN IMPERIAL BANK OF COMMERCE (CIBC))**

Having Alex at the Branding Workshop was an awesome choice I made. He was not only motivating, but challenging to every individual that was there.... His words were tugging as he challenged everyone to see within themselves that Greatness truly lies within. He was phenomenal, mind blowing and yet all with a great sense of humour. The members in the boardroom loved his personality and hung on to every word he spoke, never missing anything. **(BERLINDA BARROCKS, PRESIDENT, KAMSHUKA INC.)**

Alex gives so much more of himself to uplift others. His love for helping others is almost superhuman. His is a real hero! **(VERONICA CHAIL, HOST, OMNI TV)**

I have the pleasure to hear one of his keynote speech, and I was impressed by the delivery and the expression and presentation. And I quote "An award is not meant for you to slow down or stop, but given so that you can push forward and finish the JOB" Great words from a great person...and will definitely stick with me when I continue my push with my company and community work. **(ISAAC JR. OLOWOLAFE, PRESIDENT/CEO, DREAM FUND HOLDINGS/DREAM MAKER REALTY)**

ALEX IHAMA'S
SCHOOL OF GREATNESS

**Press Release
For Immediate Distribution**

Doors formally open to Alex Ihama's School of Greatness, the first virtual school of its kind worldwide.

August 19, 2013 – The doors to Alex Ihama's School of Greatness formally opened today to thousands of people all over the world. The first of its kind in the world, it will facilitate webinars on life and leadership skills for individuals, organizations, churches, communities, schools and governments. While it will function like conventional schools, it sets itself apart by offering courses on topics that are not usually taught in conventional schools, as well as the innovative methods of using technology to deliver their programs, and their ability to readily customize their programs to suit the needs of its students.

In the words of its Founder, Alex Ihama, who is also the President of the school, "It is high time that there is a school that offer courses and certifications on what matters most in life; and we have finally created one (a school) to do just that. At our School of Greatness, we will be teaching life skills that are expected of everyone and by everyone in the society, and yet taught by no educational institution. We will also be partnering with other schools to complement their curriculum with courses that they don't offer, but yet would empower their students to excel in school and life. Many school principals have admitted that many of their students and even some teachers struggle with procrastination, but yet offer no course on how to beat it. Now, we do."

Alex Ihama had the vision in 1999 when he claims to have been going through tumultuous moments in his life and yet could find no school that offered the courses he needed to learn the required life skills. The School of Greatness offers over three hundred courses, which includes How to Discover Life Purpose, How to Overcome Fear, How to Be Self-Motivated, How to Generate Passion, How to Turn Passion into Profit, How to Break Bad Habits, How to Increase Self-Confidence, How to Overcome Distraction, How to Beat Procrastination, How to Lead Effectively, How to Resolve Conflicts, and How to Make Effective Decisions.

Headquartered in Toronto, Canada, the School of Greatness has already partnered with some life and business experts in strategic locations around the world to offer these Life Classes, as well as certificate programs in Public Speaking, Life Coaching, Entrepreneurship and Leadership. The Leadership program is broken down into Corporate Leadership, Spiritual Leadership, Community Leadership, Youth Leadership, Professional Leadership, Academic Leadership and Political Leadership. This is a unique strategic approach of specialization in leadership development which is also being pioneered by Alex Ihama, and already making impact in institutions of higher learning.

What make the School of Greatness even more unique is that these enriching webinars will be free of charge to their students. In addition, registered students will receive a free Life Coaching session; a complimentary copy of Welcome to Greatness workbook, which is a roadmap for their individual journey through self-discovery, self-awareness and self-actualization; a lifetime membership for the School of Greatness community, where they may support each other in their individual journey; and a lifetime mentorship as well. Alex Ihama considers this part of his legacy to humanity, and called on corporations, churches, schools, government and communities to partner with the School of Greatness by hosting a campus in their locations around the world, thereby forming a support group for their people.

According to Sylvia Friedman, a Motivational Speaker, Intuitive Coach and Celebrated Author in Chicago, USA, "It is exciting to know that there is a School of Greatness. It certainly would help so many of us to have a mentor that provides all of the knowledge and strategies of life and business. I believe we all have talents and abilities that help us grow into (successful) business people. My intuition, and knowing how to develop myself, was very enlightening, and helped me to succeed. Some of us would not have worked so hard if the School of Greatness prevailed at that time." The Life Coaches, Public Speakers, School Teachers and other professionals who we spoke to applauded the School of Greatness as a unique initiative that the world desperately needs at this time.

The school has the following faculties, which are in line with what Alex Ihama referred to as the 12 Facets of Life: Personality, Leadership, Marriage, Parenting, Spirituality, Relationship, Health & Wellness, Academics, Finances, Career, Business and Life Purpose. It will also be offering Specialty Programs like How to Write a Book, How to Start a Business and How to Plan Retirement. These are available upon request from organizations, churches, communities, schools and governments, or as one-on-one coaching programs for the students.

To support the robust infrastructure for such a venture, the School of Greatness will be facilitating these specialized webinars and the certification programs for organizations, churches, communities, schools and governments, for only a fraction of the usual cost of engaging high-calibre speakers like Alex Ihama. The school will also be offering an Employee Assistance Program (EAP) for small and midsize organizations, including churches and schools that usually have none. The objective will be to empower their employees through coaching and mentoring to overcome the work and life challenges that would otherwise hinder them from maximizing their true potential.

The School of Greatness will also be soliciting for charitable donations through Alex Ihama's non-profit organization that is registered in Canada. It is The Exhortation Worldwide Community Organization, with Ontario Corporation Number 1866909, and mainly responsible for Alex Ihama's Inside Out Transformation Program. This is yet another unique initiative by Alex Ihama, with a vision "To make every inmate's detention the last one." One of his future initiatives is to have School of Greatness campuses inside prisons and detention centres all over the world.

Using a phased approach, Inside Out Transformation Program teaches inmates a particular set of Personal Proficiency Principles (PPP) through donated copies of Alex Ihama's book, Welcome to Greatness, while using life coaching by correspondence to enable them regain control of their mindset and change their behaviour inside detention centres. It will also encourage the inmates to freely participate in any of the School of Greatness programs that are required to transform their individual mindsets while being detained.

To partner with the School of Greatness, either by donating your expertise, money or hosting a campus in your corporation, church or schools, please contact:

Samantha Ihama,
Executive Director,
School of Greatness Worldwide
Phone: +1-647-272-7226
Email: registrar@schoolofgreatness.ca

About Welcome to Greatness

Welcome to Greatness is an account of a personal journey from a life of absolute self to that of absolute best; from a life of regrettable disservice to humanity to that of a passionate service for humanity.

It exposes you to the abounding strength, overwhelming intelligence and striking beauty that you likely never knew existed within you, while compelling you to face yourself and whomever or whatever you need to confront in order to live your life to the fullest.

Welcome to Greatness is a roadmap of what you require for your journey from grass to grace, from hate to love, from emptiness to fulfillment, from timidity to confidence and from fear to courage.

Welcome to Greatness is about how you may begin and sustain your own journey en route to fulfillment, from wherever you are today to where you need to be tomorrow –physically, mentally, emotionally, spiritually, relationally and financially.

Contact us if you would like to implement *Welcome to Greatness* as a curriculum in your corporation, church, government, college or organization, and to order copies of the book in bulk to initiate leadership culture in your population. Contact us too if you would like us to deliver parts of it as a keynotes or workshops.

Simply send an email to alex@alexihama.com with your curriculum, bulk order, and presentation requests.

CPSIA information can be obtained
at www.ICGtesting.com
Printed in the USA
BVHW031911311019
562619BV00001B/2/P